AMERICA'S STATES:
A CITIZENS AGENDA

1983–1984

Prepared By:

The Conference on Alternative State and Local Policies
2000 Florida Avenue, N.W.
Washington, D.C. 20009
(202) 387-6030

1983

THE CONFERENCE ON ALTERNATIVE STATE AND LOCAL POLICIES

The Conference is a national public policy center that focuses on the needs of America's state and local governments. The Conference meets these needs by developing and publicizing innovative new ideas for state and local government.

The Conference is the only national organization that develops progressive and innovative policy ideas for states, cities and towns. In the past seven years, the Conference has compiled an impressive record of initiating innovative legislation and programs with states and cities on problems such as: farmland preservation, pension fund investment, energy conservation, pay equity and comparable worth, environmental protection and economic development.

A publications program of over 100 titles, frequent regional and national conferences, numerous pieces of model legislation, an effective professional staff, a bimonthly magazine, Ways & Means, and numerous other services make up the program of the Conference.

For more information about the Conference, a sample issue of Ways & Means or our Publications Catalogue, please write to:

Lee Webb
Executive Director
2000 Florida Avenue N.W.
Washington, D.C.   20009
(202) 387-6030

AMERICA'S STATES: A CITIZENS AGENDA 1983-1984

Editors: David Jones
                      Lee Webb

Editorial Assistant: Kathleen Long

Production Coordinator: George Lehman

ISBN 0-89788-075-7

Introduction

America's state governments are at a crossroads. Their influence and power is likely to grow steadily throughout the 1980s.

President Reagan's "New Federalism" coupled with long-term political and social trends are thrusting America's states back onto the center stage of American political life. For better or worse, decisions that used to be made in the committee rooms of Congress will be made increasingly in the 50 state legislatures.

The massive cuts in federal assistance, persistently high unemployment and continuing recession have hit state budgets hard. States have been forced to lay off employees, cut needed public services and increase a variety of taxes. This fiscal crisis has required states to re-examine their programs and priorities. Interestingly, the result has been the willingness of many states to explore new directions and new programs.

This increased power of the states requires that liberals and progressives refocus their attention and resources. Since the New Deal, they have believed that the federal government was the sole instrument of social change in America. Their ideas, their lobbying and advocacy, their careers and their dreams focused on what Congress, the President, the regulatory agencies and the federal courts should do. State and local governments' potential and powers to confront the basic problems were ignored.

Until recently, states concentrated most of their attention and resources on a limited, traditional set of activities, including highway construction, prisons, public education, and railway and utility regulation. The 1980s require a broader state agenda encompassing a wide array of what had been considered national issues. Liberals and progressives can help states grapple with such "national" issues as rising health costs, air and water pollution, energy costs, tax equity, interest rates, toxics, unemployment, child care and now even nuclear arms control.

The next two years will be ones in which states make basic decisions about their role in American federalism. Will the states move squarely to confront the big problems faced by Americans or will they turn their backs, claiming that they are "powerless" to act? Many of these issues are being fought now as states grapple with the effects of the massive cutbacks in federal aid, with the weakening or elimination of many federal regulatory programs, and the nationwide recession.

The 1982 elections brought hundreds of progressive legislators and a number of activist governors into positions of power. Many of the successful legislators ran on a program of innovation and thoughtful reform. America's States: A Citizens Agenda 1983-1984 was written and prepared for this new generation of state legislators, statewide officials and governors who are now leaders of their states. Based largely on the highly successful Conference publication, The Issues of 1982: A Briefing Book, prepared for state candidates in 1982, America's States outlines a detailed progressive agenda for state action.

America's States: A Citizens Agenda offers the reader detailed analysis and exciting new ideas on 36 of the critical issues now confronting state government. These briefing papers are grouped in 10 broad sections which include: Economic Development, Natural Resources and Environment, Human Services, Crime, the Governmental Process, Consumer Issues, Labor and Work, Education, Civil and Human Rights, and National Issues.

Each of the 36 issues is covered in a five page briefing paper. The first page presents basic facts and statistics on the issue. Pages two and three describe the major problems, controversies and policy choices surrounding the issue, the fourth page outlines a concrete program for state action, including legislation, and the final page describes organizations and publications that can be additional resources.

The individuals who contributed to this book by writing individual briefing papers are some of the most intelligent and brighest people in the country. Their knowledge of their issues, their experience in policy analysis and their understanding of what states can do about the issues makes this book a unique and extraordinary resource. Their willingness to commit the time and energy to prepare these remarkable papers is enormously appreciated.

America's States: A Citizens Agenda is one of a wealth of resources that the Conference on Alternative State and Local Policies makes available to state and local officials, citizens and civic organizations. Our recent publications catalogue details over 35 books the Conference has published recently. And our bimonthly magazine, Ways and Means, is read by over 3,000 state and local public officials.

The next two years will be very important to America's states. The legislatures are faced with extremely difficult problems. Hopefully, the new generation of state officials coming to power in the states will be able to make substantial use of this book and the ideas presented.

Lee Webb
Executive Director

Table of Contents

INTRODUCTION   i

ECONOMIC DEVELOPMENT

    Banking   3
        by Larry Swift
    Community Economic Development   9
        by Robert Zdenek
    Cooperatives   15
        by Ann Evans
    High Technology   21
        by Fred Branfman
    Pension Fund Investment   27
        by Thomas Leatherwood
    Plant Closings   33
        by David Jones and William Schweke
    Small Business   39
        by Derek Hansen

NATURAL RESOURCES AND ENVIRONMENT

    Farm and Food Policy   47
        by Joe Belden
    Environmental Protection   53
        by Peter Lafen
    Nuclear Energy   59
        by William Jordan
    Energy Conservation   65
        by Richard Munson
    Toxics   71
        by James Lewis and Ken Silver
    Water and Sewers   77
        by Edward Hopkins and David Zwick

HUMAN SERVICES

    Child Care   85
        by Barbara Bode and Lori Weinstein
    Child Support Enforcement   91
        by Worth Kitson Cooley
    The Elderly   97
        by Joanna Chusid
    Health Care   103
        by Anthony Robbins

Housing   109
    by Leonard Goldberg and Marilee Hanson

CRIME

    Criminal Justice   117
        by Elliott Currie
    Handgun Control   123
        by Donald Fraher

THE GOVERNMENTAL PROCESS

    Block Grants   131
        by Barbara Pape
    Corruption and Waste   137
        by Peter Manikas

CONSUMER ISSUES

    Consumer Protection   145
        by Richard Spohn
    Insurance   151
        by Robert Hunter
    Tax Reform   157
        by David Wilhelm
    Utilities   163
        by Jeff Brummer

LABOR AND WORK

    Labor Legislation   171
        by William Schweke
    Public Employees   177
        by Linda Lampkin
    Workplace Safety and Health   183
        by John Froines

EDUCATION

    Public Education   191
        by Andrea DiLorenzo and Linda Tarr-Whelan
    Students   197
        by David Jones

CIVIL AND HUMAN RIGHTS

    Citizens with Disabilities   205
        by Deborah Kaplan
    Civil Rights   211
        by Michael Samuels
    Women   217
        by Linda Tarr-Whelan

NATIONAL ISSUES

Constitutional Amendments   225
     by Andrea DiLorenzo and Linda Tarr-Whelan
Nuclear Weapons Freeze   231
     by Victoria Baldwin, Ann Cahn and
     Lou Kerestesy

LIST OF CONTRIBUTORS   237

Economic Development

Banking

BACKGROUND FACTS

The American economy becomes more nationally and globally interdependent every year. Capital flows further, faster and with less public accountability than ever before.

States and communities are increasingly vulnerable to these flows of capital. Banks, insurance companies and money market funds are soaking up deposits in a state and are exporting them as loans to other states or even to other countries. Disinvestment -- originally a neighborhood problem -- is now a state and regional problem.

Money market funds are a big part of the problem. According to Angelo Bianchi of the Conference of State Bank Supervisors, "Money market mutual funds are bleeding numerous state and local communities of their economic life blood." These "massive shifts of assets have jeopardized the ability of many financial institutions to meet the investment and credit needs of their communities."

On interstate banking, Mr. Bianchi commented, "I don't think removing the barriers (from) Citibank is going to help me in my state. All they are going to do is take money out of my state and invest it in Eurodollars or in Zaire or maybe even in Iran."

The American banking industry is undergoing massive changes that are weakening the ability of states to act. The savings and loan industry is in crisis. Banks and savings and loans are being rapidly deregulated. Non-banks are moving into banking. Banks are being consolidated and merged at an increasing rate. The federal government is preempting state banking regulation and laws. Banking is moving across state lines. And new technologies, especially automatic teller machines, promise major changes.

The loss of state control over credit cost and availability comes at a time when states' credit needs are intensified by the shift of public responsibility for economic problems from the federal to the state level and to the private sector.

Federal program cutbacks, coupled with federally-induced erosion of the state tax base and rising state unemployment costs require states to expand control of public and private debt financing mechanisms to meet fundamental social and economic development objectives.

THE PROBLEM

The ability of the states to regulate banking is severe
attack. The nation's dual banking system, under which the
state and federal governments enjoyed competitive equality in
chartering and regulating financial institutions for the past
hundred years, is rapidly coming to an end. If states are to
protect and enhance their economic and social interests, a
great deal of creativity will be needed over the next few
years to shape the changing banking system to meet tomorrow's
credit needs.

The cost and availability of debt capital to finance public,
private and consumer needs is determined increasingly in the
board rooms of nationwide banking entities and the offices of
the federal banking regulators. The ability of state legislatures to insure the availability and affordability of
credit for housing, agriculture, industrial and commercial
development and consumer purchases has steadily diminished.

The savings and loan industry is in crisis. Savings
and loan associations are failing at a hectic pace. Eighty-
three percent experienced losses in the first half of 1982.
Last year the Federal Savings and Loan Insurance Corporation
merged 75 savings and loans out of existence. A total of
787 savings and loans went out of existence in 1981 and 1982.
Twenty savings and loans have been merged across state lines
and other savings and loans have been merged into commercial
bank holding companies. Those savings and loans that survive
are likely to be indistinguishable from commercial banks.

Thirty-five banks were closed by the Federal Deposit
Insurance Corporation (F.D.I.C.) in 1982. The F.D.I.C.
chairman, William Issac, says we should not "be surprised if
the number of failures increases in 1983."

Since, proportionally, state chartered institutions tend
to be smaller and the smaller institutions are failing more
rapidly, the states' role will diminish in the years ahead.

The U. S. Congress and the federal regulators are preempting state banking law and regulation. A recent federal
law eliminated state controls on interest rates (though the
states can override this). The Federal Reserve Board now
sets reserve requirements for all financial institutions,
including state chartered banks and savings and loans. The
Supreme Court has ruled the Federal Home Loan Bank Board's
regulation permitting federal savings and loans to enforce
the due-on-sale clause in mortgages is superior to state law.

Congress will likely enact major banking legislation in
the near future which will further deregulate the banking
industry. Where state law is not directly preempted, de
facto preemption is likely because state chartered lenders

-4-

will convert to federal charters if the states don't similarly deregulate.

The growth of nationwide banking will also undermine state regulation. Financial institutions in over 30 states are currently participating in multi-state automatic teller machine (ATM) networks. Negotiations are underway to form nationwide ATM networks, according to Business Week. The banking industry and federal regulators are lobbying hard to eliminate federal prohibitions on interstate banking -- an outcome that appears inevitable.

In addition, the emergence of non-regulated banking entities (for example, money market mutual funds, Sears, Merrill Lynch, National Steel Corporation and Prudential-Bache) pose great problems for states since these corporations operate across state lines with neither state nor federal regulation.

The money market mutual funds and other recent entrants into the financing industry operate with significant competitive advantages because Congress and federal regulators have chosen not to regulate them.

Because the changes in the banking industry are so radical and being made so swiftly, policy responses have by and large been piecemeal and incidental.

At the federal level, the Community Reinvestment Act (CRA), which was passed in the 1970s, has been the most significant response. The CRA imposed on banks and savings and loan asso- ciations the responsibility to meet the credit needs of local areas from which the deposits were taken. Although CRA isn't specific enough, it has been a valuable tool in improving credit availability in neighborhoods. In addition, numerous states have implemented community reinvestment legislation or regulations.

Another state response has been to create new public sources of financing to meet credit needs within the states. At least 35 states have used housing finance agencies and mortgage revenue bonds for single and multi-family housing. Commercial revitalization, plant expansions and new factories have been financed by industrial revenue bonds in many states. Some states, particularly Massachusetts, have established state agencies with bonding authority to finance economic development. California has recently set up an Alternative Energy System Financing Authority to provide credit for renewable energy systems development.

Some states, such as California, have been actively seeking ways to employ public pension funds to achieve state economic and social objectives. Illinois, in 1982, passed legislation to facilitate more effective uses of public pension funds.

WHAT STATES CAN DO

Redirect Banking Law

° States should enact state Community Reinvestment Acts requiring financial institutions to help meet the credit needs of their local communities. California, Massachusetts, Ohio and other states have such laws and regulations.

° States should establish linked deposit programs under which deposits of state funds are placed with financial institutions committed to lending funds to meet specified credit needs of the state's citizens. Missouri and Illinois have such programs.

° States that permit out-of-state banks to establish banking facilities should pass legislation to ensure that the out-of-state banks meet the credit needs within the state.

Alternative Credit Providing Institutions

° States should establish a state-owned bank and permit the establishment of municipally-owned banks. A public bank, like the Bank of North Dakota can help insure that the state's credit needs are being met.

° States should establish development finance agencies with authority to raise capital through issuing bonds. Thirty-nine states now have housing finance agencies to help meet various housing credit needs.

° States should use public pension funds to help meet credit and investment needs. In addition to giving legislative direction to pension fund trustees, states should establish risk reduction mechanisms (such as loan guarantees) to facilitate investment in higher risk ventures and secondary market mechanisms to package smaller loans for sale to the funds.

° States should help capitalize development banks like the South Shore National Bank of Chicago, which provides credit in an inner-city neighborhood to help meet unmet or undermet credit needs to facilitate community development.

Pressure on Federal Government

° States should lobby Congress to reassert control of the Federal Reserve Board (FRB). The FRB is a creature of Congress but operates independently.

FOR FURTHER INFORMATION

Publications

"CRA: A Tool for Attracting Private Financing of Neighborhood Revitalization", Woodstock Institute, Larry Swift, 1981, free. Explains the Community Reinvestment Act and how it can be used to stimulate revitalization.

Evaluation of the Illinois Neighborhood Development Corporation. Summary Report, Woodstock Institute, Dennis Marino, et al, 1982. Evaluated community development and financial performance of South Shore Bank of Chicago and its affiliates.

Investment Targeting -- A Wisconsin Case Study, Donald Smart, et al, 1979, Wisconsin Center for Public Policy. Develops a model for the investment of public pension funds to help meet state economic development goals.

Pension Funds and Economic Renewal, Lawrence Litvak, 1981. Conference on Alternative State and Local Policies, $14.95.

Selective Deposits of Public Funds, Leonard Rubinowitz, 1977, Woodstock Institute, $3.00. An analysis of state and local programs which link deposits of public money to reinvestment activities of banks.

Social Investments and the Law: The Case for Alternative Investment, 1980, Conference on Alternative State and Local Policies, $6.95.

Strategic Investment: An Alternative for Public Funds, 1980 Conference on Alternative State and Local Policies, $5.95.

Organizations

CENTER FOR COMMUNITY CHANGE, Neighborhood Revitalization Project, 1000 Wisconsin Avenue, N.W., Washington, D.C. 20007. Allen Fishbein, Director. Research and technical assistance organization which publishes periodic legislative alerts on banking and neighborhood reinvestment issues.

CONFERENCE ON ALTERNATIVE STATE AND LOCAL POLICIES, 2000 Florida Avenue, N.W., Washington, D.C. 20009. Lee Webb, Director. Publishes studies on banking and public investment policy and periodic updates on new state and local legislation.

WOODSTOCK INSTITUTE, 417 S. Dearborn Street, Chicago, IL 60605. Larry Swift, President. Research and technical assistance organization focusing on neighborhood reinvestment and banking issues.

Prepared by Larry Swift.

Community Economic Development

BACKGROUND FACTS

America's neighborhoods and communities are in trouble. Inner city neighborhoods, rural counties and old industrial cities face persistent unemployment, poor public services, collapsing infrastructure, abandoned buildings and few financial resources.

Unemployment nationally among black youths is in excess of 50 percent. In Miami and in some other areas, the unemployment rate for black males is 75 percent. The adult unemployment rate on the large Navajo reservation in the Southwest is around 70 percent.

In the stricken city of Youngstown, Ohio, 1300 people applied for 50 minimum wage jobs at the Bob Evans Farm Sausage Restaurant. In Nashville, Tennessee, 40,000 individuals applied for 800 jobs at a Japanese electronics plant.

The American job market is undergoing a rapid and fundamental transition from labor-intensive, heavy industries toward capital-intensive industries requiring highly trained, skilled workers.

The restructuring of the American economy has had an enormous impact on communities dependent on heavy industry. Plant closings forced cities to slash public services. And recent increases in industrial output will not significantly reduce the level of unemployment in these communities.

America's antiquated and decaying physical infrastructure, a necessity for economic growth, is a tremendous obstacle to economic growth. Roads, water systems, sewers, transportation lines and physical plants are declining at a faster rate than they are being replaced.

Distressed communities also suffer from low rates of business formation and high rates of business failures. The business failure rate in distressed communities is in excess of 80 percent, due primarily to a business person's difficulty in obtaining conventional financing and their lack of management experience.

THE PROBLEM

Community economic development is a strategy to revitalize communities and neighborhoods, involving residents, local government and the private sector. The goal is increased economic activity. Since many of these communities have limited financial resources, outside financial resources, for example, federal, state and private funds are needed to spur long-term economic revitalization.

Even in a period of economic growth, distressed communities get fewer opportunities and less growth than other parts of the country. These problems, compounded by a lack of local ownership and poor internal economic multipliers in the community, lead to disinvestment and decline.

Community problems are accentuated by the decline of physical infrastructure -- not only in the Northeast and Mid-west but throughout the country. Lack of planning, time delays, and the exorbitant costs of physical infrastructure projects delay or negate private economic development initiatives.

Although federal community economic development efforts are being drastically reduced as a result of the President's "New Federalism" program, innovative state efforts for community economic development are increasing. One of the most exciting state community economic develoment initiatives, the Community Development Finance Corporation (CDFC) of Massachusetts, was established in 1976 to provide venture capital financing for small businesses in distressed communities. Wisconsin, Florida, Minnesota, Illinois, Alaska and California have since initiatied similar programs.

Many innovative programs originated as state efforts to broaden their economic development strategy. States moved from simply "smokestack chasing" to more comprehensive development strategies emphasizing job creation through small business activities -- the major economic sector that creates new jobs that are filled by low income people.

Powerful competitive factors, labor and capital market barriers, and federal policies prevent communities and neigh-borhoods from improving their own economy. Obviously, some communities would not be experiencing unemployment, poor physical infrastructure and high business failure rate if there were not significant economic barriers to economic

growth. These barriers include: lack of information for
judging sound business opportunities; the cost of preparing
and obtaining financing for businesses; risk aversion of
lending institutions; lack of training for current and future
jobs; and limited placement efforts for job openings.

Many conservatives argue that economic development and
job creation are the responsibility of the private sector
alone. They argue that only the private sector creates new
jobs. They fail to recognize that there are significant
barriers to private sector development in certain areas, such
as declining infrastructure and perceived high risk. In
addition, distressed communities have a limited private
sector that cannot effectively mobilize the capital, assistance
and management expertise needed to address overwhelming
problems and issues.

Community economic development programs are also criti-
cized as being part of the "urban renewal" activities of the
late 1960's. Critics argue that urban renewal and public
development activites have exacerbated development problems
and wasted considerable amounts of taxpayer dollars because
they have not created enough employment and ownership opportunities for low-income residents. Yet community economic
development is actually the opposite of large-scale inefficient
urban renewal efforts. It is predicated upon the involvement
of local residents and the targeting of scarce development
resources for small-scale projects with long-term impacts.

Both conservatives and progressives have viewed some
government funded community economic develoment efforts as
"pork barrel" programs. Critics argue that scarce federal and
state dollars are used to finance projects in areas that are
not distressed -- for example, 85 percent of the U.S. population
lives in areas eligible for Economic Development Administration
(EDA) financing. Thus, some contend, community economic
development programs are too costly, even if they have positive
results.

Critics fail to recognize that community economic development reduces individual and community dependency and builds
greater self-reliance within the communities. Increasing the
dependency of a community on the other hand, not only requires
more public dollars but also squanders valuable human resources.
Community economic development therefore, is often the most
cost-effective way of revitalizing distressed communities.

WHAT STATES CAN DO

Equity and Debt Capital for Community Economic Development

° States should establish Community Development Finance Corporations (CDFCs). The Massachusetts legislature created
  such a corporation in 1976 with $10 million of assets to
  invest in community owned businesses development in distressed
  communities.

° States should establish Community Development Finance Author-
  ities (CDFA). Wisconsin signed into law such an agency on
  May 6, 1982. The Wisconsin CDFA will be capitalized by
  selling tax credits to corporations and individuals along
  the line of the Neighborhood Assistance Act (NAA).

° States should establish loan programs to provide start-up
  costs to Community Development Corporations, such as the
  program of the Florida Department of Community Affairs
  which provides low-interest loans on a competitive basis
  to business and physical development projects submitted by
  CDCs that create job opportunities for low-income residents.

Technical Assistance and Administrative Support

° States should establish centers to provide technical assis-
  tance to new and expanding small businesses, such as the
  Community Economic Develoment and Assistance Corporation
  (CEDAC), a sister corporation of the CDFC in Massachusetts.

° States should establish grant programs to provide administrative support. The Florida Department of Community
  Affairs provides administrative grants of up to $100,000
  to between 10 to 20 urban and rural CDCs

Other State Develoment Programs That Can Stimulate Community
Economic Development

° States should provide tax credits for individual and corporate contributions made to neighborhood assistance or
  commercial improvements projects. Seven states (Pennsylvania,
  Missouri, Indiana, Michigan, Delaware, Virginia and Florida)
  have passed such legislation.

° States should establish corporations that encourage capital
  investment in small, growth-oriented firms. Both Connecticut
  New Project Development Corporation (CNPDC) and the Indiana
  Corporation for Innovative Development (ICID) encourage
  capital investment in small, growth-oriented firms that
  cannot obtain conventional financing.

FOR FURTHER INFORMATION

Publications

Community Development Corporations and State Development Policy: Potential Partnerships, Benson Roberts, Robert Zdenek and William Bivens. National Congress for Community Economic Development, $15.00. Explores how CDCs and state governments can develop innovative development and job creation programs.

Expanding the Opportunity to Produce: Revitalizing the American Economy Through New Enterprise Development edited by Robert Friedman and William Schweke, $20.00 from the Corporation for Enterprise Development. A compilation of articles discussing innovative strategies for economic revitalization.

Putting America Back To Work: What States and Cities Can Do, by William Schweke and Lee Webb, $6.95 from the Conference on Alternative State and Local Policies.

States and Communities: The Challenge for Economic Action, National Congress for Community Economic Development, 1983.

Organizations

CONFERENCE ON ALTERNATIVE STATE AND LOCAL POLICIES, 2000 Florida Avenue, N.W., Washington, D.C. 20009 (202) 387-6030, Lee Webb, Executive Director.

CORPORATION FOR ENTERPRISE DEVELOPMENT, 1211 Connecticut Ave. N.W., Suite 710 A, Washington, D.C., 20036 (202) 293-7963, Robert Friedman, President. Publishes books on enterprise development, and a newsletter, The Entrepreneurial Economy.

COUNSEL FOR COMMUNITY DEVELOPMENT, INC., 10 Concord Ave., Cambridge, MA, 02138, (617) 492-5461, Belden Daniels, President. Specializes in policy research and studies in economic development.

NATIONAL CONGRESS FOR COMMUNITY ECONOMIC DEVELOPMENT, 2025 Eye St., N.W., #901, Washington, D.C. 20006, (202) 659-8411, Robert Zdenek, President. A membership association of community-based development organizations that publishes a monthly newsletter, Resources; undertakes policy analysis and research; and prepares handbooks on topics such as syndication strategies and fundraising.

NATIONAL ECONOMIC DEVELOPMENT AND LAW CENTER, 1950 Addison Street, Berkeley, CA, 94704, (415) 548-2460, David Kirkpatrick, Executive Director. Provides extensive technical assistance in business packaging, legal and organizational issues.

Prepared by Robert Zdenek.

Cooperatives

Many American families believe they are economically worse off now than they were ten years ago. Food prices, interest rates and energy prices have doubled.

Americans are looking for alternatives and many have turned to cooperatives. In fact, 25 percent of all Americans or a member of their household belong to a cooperative.

If Americans had more co-ops available to them or knew more about them, the co-ops they would be most interested in joining, in order of preference, are food (54 percent), health care (27 percent), housing (19 percent), energy (18 percent), auto repair (18 percent), and child care (8 percent).

In 1979, nearly 3,000 cooperative food stores and buying clubs were retailing food to their member owners and others. Co-op customers save 21.7 percent on food costs.

Health care co-op costs range up to 40 percent below the national average. The Group Health Cooperative of Puget Sound, for example, reports its average cost per prescription was $2.02 compared with an average in the Pacific Northwest area of $4.80.

Fuel oil co-ops, especially popular in the Northeast, save members' money for heating. The co-ops offer fuel oil at eight to 12 cent per gallon less than prevailing retail prices. Other energy co-ops help members buy and install conservation materials and solar equipment.

Housing co-ops offer home ownership opportunities to those who can least afford it. Limited equity housing co-ops offer the greatest savings; initially, they are an average of five to 10 percent less than comparable housing. Over time this savings increases to up to 50 percent.

Cooperatives are proven tools of self-reliance and community-controlled economic development. Co-ops can be the vehicles for new commercial businesses, creating jobs and improving the goods and services that will rebuild and stabilize neighborhoods.

Capital to start cooperatives used to be a barrier. But in 1978 Congress created the National Consumer Cooperative Bank. As of June 1982, the Bank had million in capital available for loans.

THE PROBLEM

Cooperatives are businesses owned and controlled by the people who use them. They arise to fill the economic needs of consumers, workers or the community. Cooperatives are a relatively small segment of the economy -- in most areas of operation they have a limited market share -- but they have a significant impact in those areas and among those people affected by them.

Legally, co-ops are hybrid corporations falling in between nonprofit and for-profit corporations. Co-ops operate on a not-for-profit basis -- service, not profit, is their motivating force. Essentially, co-ops are nonprofit corporations that sell stock and distribute profits to their member-owners.

Although cooperatives offer consumers, workers and their communities a tremendous opportunity, numerous obstacles block the survival and expansion of cooperatives. Specifically, co-ops have faced two recurring problems: lack of access to adequate credit and to technical and managerial assistance. Private financing sources have been reluctant to provide credit because the corporate structure of a cooperative is unfamiliar to them: (1) co-ops have no identifiable majority stockholder that can be held accountable and (2) co-ops are not-for-profit businesses. In addition, publicly funded technical and managerial assistance programs are designed for profit-oriented businesses and rarely available to service-oriented cooperative businesses.

A score of serious, related problems have compounded the effects of co-ops' lack of accessible credit and technical assistance. These problems, which create a difficult environment for cooperatives, include:

° The lack of legislatively mandated state agencies that have specific statutory authority and advocacy duties for cooperatives.

° The lack of public education programs that provide consumer awareness about cooperative businesses and train their future managers.

As a result, little of the normal support network so crucial to the survival and success of corporate enterprise exists for co-ops. State policies that are aimed at stimulating business, housing or health care often exclude co-ops. State regulation often either ignores co-ops' special needs or is openly hostile to their corporate structure and their needs.

Despite the problems, cooperatives have long been a part of the American scene because they offer so many advantages. Some of these advantages include:

° Co-ops save money. They are self-help efforts. They distribute their earnings back to members on the basis of patronage, not investment. In the case of housing cooperatives, the absence of the monthly cost of the owner's profit inherent in most rental projects, the tax benefits, and minimal maintenance costs contribute to the affordability. The increases in monthly housing cost are limited to actual increases in operating costs because the co-op is not-for-profit.

° Co-ops are often the only way a neighborhood in the inner city or in rural areas can get the basic necessities. At one time, residents in Watts, California, had no supermarket within three square miles. Now, Watts residents own and control their own co-op food market.

° Co-ops provide a training ground for members in democracy and public participation. Such training of a citizenry is critical to the maintenance of a pluralistic democracy. For example, Alabaman black farmers went on to field a slate of candidates for county government after they had successfully organized their marketing cooperative. Leaders of local food and housing cooperatives have frequently stepped from co-op boards to the local planning commission or city council.

° Co-ops provide constant public education. Food co-ops in Berkeley and Chicago have pioneered the use of ingredient labeling, net weight listing, nutritional labeling and unit pricing. They even staff their retail stores with full-time home economists to answer questions from consumers and to perform educational demonstrations.

In general, the cooperative is the only method of organization of industrial enterprise that guarantees that more regional income stays within the region. Cooperatives also contribute to regional self-sufficiency and to decentralization of wealth and of economic organization.

Small business organizations sometimes argue that cooperatives have an unfair competitive edge because they do not have to make a profit. Conservative taxpayer associations argue that cooperatives do not pay taxes (this is because net profit for tax purposes in cooperatives is computed after the distribution of the patronage refund). But any business that wants to redistribute profit or overcharge to customers on this basis, can receive the same tax treatment.

WHAT STATES CAN DO

General

° States should establish "Task Forces on Cooperative Development" to bring together state officials and cooperative leaders to develop a state action plan for cooperative development.

° States should enact a separate "cooperative" section in their corporation code. The 1982 California bill is an excellent national model.

° States should modify their security laws to meet the unique needs of cooperatives as New Mexico did in 1982.

Education

° States should require their state colleges and universities to create programs to train managers, staff and boards of directors of cooperatives.

° States should establish educational programs for cooperatives, assisting them with accounting, management, business planning, financing and other needed skills.

Housing

° States should enact general legislation, similar to that in the District of Columbia, limiting cooperative and condominium conversion of older buildings to give existing tenants the first right to buy the building or individual units.

° States should enact legislation that defines "limited equity" housing co-ops. Subsequent legislation and regulations should give preference to such cooperatives.

° States should enact legislation making housing cooperatives eligible for mortgage financing through tax-exempt bonds.

Financing

° States should use escheat funds from cooperatives for continued cooperative development. In many states unclaimed co-op members' shares and dividends return (escheat) to the state after several years.

° States should allow credit unions to lend to co-ops. Many credit unions make consumer loans to co-op members but not directly to co-ops themselves.

° States should allow transfer payment reinvestment (from public assistance payments or unemployment compensation) for those who are trying to start a new cooperative business.

FOR FURTHER INFORMATION

Publications

The Board of Directors of Cooperatives, 1976, Garoyan &
Mohn, The Regents of the University of California, c/o
Associated Cooperatives Resource Center, 4801 Central Avenue,
Richmond, CA 94804.

Building Cooperatives in California: A Model for State
Action, Leonard Goldberg, 1983. Conference on Alternative
State and Local Policies. ($6.95/$13.95 institutions)

Community Energy Cooperatives: How to Organize, Finance,
and Manage Them, 1982. Conference on Alternative State and
Local Policies. ($9.95/$19.95 institutions)

An Introduction to Cooperative Conversions, 1980, State
of California, Department of Housing and Community Development,
921 Tenth St., Room 102, Sacramento, CA 95814.

We Own It: Starting and Managing Co-ops, Collectives,
and Employee Owned Ventures, Honigsberg, Kamoroff and Beatty,
Bell Springs Publishing, Laytonville, CA 95454.

Organizations

CONFERENCE ON ALTERNATIVE STATE AND LOCAL POLICIES, Co-op
Development and Assistance Project, 2000 Florida Avenue, N.W.,
Washington, D.C. 20009 (202) 387-6030. Provides technical
assistance to low-income cooperatives.

COOPERATIVE DEVELOPMENT PROGRAM, California State Department
of Consumer Affairs, 1020 N St., Rm. 501, Sacramento, CA
95814 (916) 322-7674. Publications and technical assistance.

COOPERATIVE LEAGUE OF THE USA, 1828 L Street, N.W., Washington,
D.C., 20036 (202) 872-0550. Umbrella trade association for
producer and consumer cooperatives.

INDUSTRIAL COOPERATIVE ASSOCIATION, 2161 Massachusetts Avenue,
Cambridge, MA, 02140 (617) 547-4245. Helps obtain financing,
marketing and technical assistance to industrial cooperatives.

NATIONAL ASSOCIATION OF HOUSING COOPERATIVES, 2501 M Street,
N.W., Suite 451, Washington, D.C., 20037 (202) 887-0706.

NATIONAL CONSUMER COOPERATIVE BANK, 1630 Connecticut Avenue,
Washington, D.C., 20009 (202) 745-4630. Provides loans and
technical assistance to cooperatives.

Prepared by Ann Evans.

High Technology

The basic cause of many states' economic problems is our declining investment in industrial innovation and productivity. This problem is at root a cause of high unemployment, plant closings and even declining state revenue.

For well-known reasons -- rising energy prices, tough international competition, poor corporate management, the export of capital abroad and increased military spending -- American corporations have been investing less in new product and process innovation than ever before. Evidence of this economic decline include:

° Lower growth in productivity. Manufacturing productivity has dropped from a 3.2 percent growth rate in 1948-65 to a 2.4 percent increase in 1965-73 to a 1.8 percent growth rate from 1973-78 to a 0.8 percent drop in 1978-80.

° Weak international competitiveness. Between 1973 and 1979, the United States ranked 10th in productivity improvement among international competitors. Our overall productivity growth of 0.9 percent during this period lagged behind Sweden (1.8 percent), Italy (2.4 percent), Canada (2.5 percent), Japan (3.8 percent), Denmark (4.1 percent), Netherlands (4.2 percent), France (4.8 percent), Belgium (4.9 percent) and West Germany (5.0 percent).

° Inadequate growth in real income. Median family income grew at a 37.6 percent real average rate from 1950-59, 33.9 percent from 1960 to 1969, 6.7 percent from 1970-79, and actually declined 5.5 percent in 1980.

Economists agree that American business has drastically cut back in the amount of funds invested in product and process innovation, successful technologies and long-term product development. Only 35 percent of aggregate business non-residential investment today is devoted to new products and process, down from 75-80 percent in the 1950s and 1960s, according to Data Resources, Inc.

THE PROBLEM

The cause of our decreased investment in successful technologies and productivity improvements is poor use of existing
capital, not a "capital shortage."

Large, resource-dependent, established corporations and
businesses have a far stronger political voice than new, high
technology, relatively resource-efficient, growing industries.
As a result, many corporate and government decisions affecting
credit allocation during the past decade have been skewed toward
wasteful uses of capital. Examples include:

° An enormous increase in capital devoted to new mergers and
  acquisitions, rather than productive investment in new
  technologies and processes. Mergers and acquisitions soaked
  up $82 billion in 1981, up from $44 billion in 1980.

° Major misallocations of capital by large auto and steel companies. General Motors, Ford and Chrysler have consistently
  misjudged their markets, allowing the Japanese to capture a
  20 percent market-share. U.S. Steel used its scarce capital
  to diversify out of the steel industry, particularly in its
  successful purchase of Marathon Oil. It did not use that
  capital to invest in new product and process technology as
  their Japanese competitors did.

° Increased military spending. This has diverted large
  amounts of investment capital away from badly needed innovation in our civilian industries, and as importantly,
  away from civilian industrial research and top engineers.

° Deregulation of oil and natural gas prices. This leads
  to the diversion of hundreds of billions of dollars from
  the general civilian economy to the treasuries of major oil
  and natural gas companies. These firms have tended to
  invest this capital in traditional resource exploitation,
  with which they are familiar, rather than in the unfamiliar,
  new and growing high technology sectors.

° Misguided tax policies. These include continuing tax breaks
  for the synthetic fuel, nuclear power, oil and gas industries,
  and recent accelerated tax depreciation and "safe harbor"
  tax leasing schemes. All divert investment funds to "shelters"
  rather than productive investments.

The Reagan administration's "Accelerated Cost Recovery
System" (ACRS) gives increased tax benefits for investment
in industrial real estate and actually decreases benefits
for the short-lived equipment used by most high technology
firms. "Safe harbor" leasing was specifically designed to
aid older firms and is of little benefit to growing industries.

Current national policies have greatly exacerbated these problems. Big federal deficits leading to high interest rates have produced a "corporate liquidity crisis" unprecedented since the Depression. Business today is spending most of its revenue to service short-term debt, pay salaries, replace vital equipment and meet other day-to-day needs. Short-term debt service is far too high.

One key to restoring economic health and increasing employment is to increase our investment in industrial innovation and productivity. Present policies encouraging nonproductive capital and credit allocation need to be changed. New policies are needed to encourage productive investment. These policies could include:

° Eliminate policies encouraging unproductive investment. We need to reduce unproductive military spending; use the Credit Control Act to discourage mergers and acquisitions; and eliminate tax breaks to the synthetic fuel, nuclear power, oil, natural gas and other older industries, focusing on drastically revising the ACRS act and eliminating the "safe harbor" leasing breaks.

° Promote policies encouraging productive activity. We need to encourage research and development into new, civilian sector, product and process developments; support education and job-training programs designed to equip workers for the new technological economy; support export promotion as an alternative to restricting free trade; and encourage programs designed to give employees a greater say and ownership in the firms within which they work.

° Promote policies targeted to key sectors. We need to target capital and other benefits to certain key sectors, particularly those targeted for development by strong international competitors like Japan, France and West Germany. For example, we need support for tax policies to aid semiconductor, computer, biotechnology and other key high technology sectors which have become the driving force of our economic growth. Where tax policies are insufficient to guarantee economic health, we must consider a more direct government role in providing low-cost capital -- for example, through a national "Innovation Finance Corporation."

WHAT STATES CAN DO

Promote Productive Investment of Pension and Tax Monies

° States should enact legislation creating state venture
  capital corporations similar to the Connecticut New Product
  Development Corporation to make equity investments in new
  high technology companies that will expand the state's
  jobs.

° States should eliminate barriers preventing their public
  and private pension funds from investing some of their
  capital in high technology growth firms.

° States should promote tax policies designed to encourage
  productive investment, such as the California law proposed
  by Governor Brown that eliminated the capital gains tax
  dividends paid by smaller firms and made up the revenue
  loss by increasing taxes on gold, paintings and other
  collectibles.

Promote Research and Development

° States should set up joint research programs between industry
  and universities, as California did with its MICRO project
  at the University of California. The project provides
  joint one-to-one matching grants for research and development
  projects in microelectronics and computer research.

Promote Technological Literacy and High Technology Job Training

° States should develop policies which emphasize equipping
  young people and older workers with the skills they need
  to survive in today's technological workplace. California
  passed in 1982 a $26 million "Investment in People" program,
  which funds teacher training and retraining in math, science
  and computer studies; high technology, employment-based
  job training at the community colleges; increased support
  for engineering and computer science faculty at universities;
  and high technology training in existing apprenticeship
  programs.

FOR FURTHER INFORMATION

Publications

Expanding the Opportunity to Produce: Revitalizing the
American Economy Through New Enterprise Development, edited
by Robert Friedman and William Schweke, Corporation for
Enterprise Development, 1981. Available for $19.95.

Putting America Back to Work: What States and Cities
Can Do, William Schweke and Lee Webb, 1982. Available for
$6.95 from the Conference on Alternative State and Local
Policies.

State Policy Options for High Technology Promotion,
Governor's Office of Policy and Planning, State House,
Trenton, NJ 08625.

Technology Innovation and Regional Economic Development,
Office of Technology Assessment, 1983. Available for $4.50
from Superintendent of Documents, U.S. Government Printing
Office, Washington, D.C. 20402. Document #052-003-00912-0.

Organizations

CALIFORNIA WORKSITE EDUCATION AND TRAINING ACT, Steve
Dusche, 800 Capitol Mall, Sacramento, CA 95814 (916) 323-3006.
An innovative job training program requiring an employment
commitment to hire and substantial on-the-job training prior
to funding training programs.

NATIONAL COMMISSION ON INDUSTRIAL INNOVATION, 1125 W. 6th
Street, Suite 300, Los Angeles, CA 90017 (213) 481-2270.

NATIONAL GOVERNORS ASSOCIATION TASKFORCE ON TECHNOLOGICAL
INNOVATION, Charlyn Cowan, 444 N. Capitol Street, N.W.,
Washington, D.C. 20001. The NGA Taskforce on Technological
Innovation has compiled a booklet listing major state
efforts around the nation to promote industrial innovation.

NEW YORK OFFICE OF POLICY DEVELOPMENT, Office of the Governor,
State Capitol, Albany, NY 12224.

OFFICE OF TECHNOLOGY ASSESSMENT, U. S. Congress, Washington,
D.C. 20510 (202) 224-8996.

Prepared by Fred Branfman.

Pension Fund Investment

BACKGROUND FACTS

Pension funds now have enormous influence in the American economy. Their influence will continue to grow rapidly.

Total pension fund assets are now more than $800 billion. These assets are held in state and local public employee pension funds and two kinds of private funds: employer/employee jointly-administered funds; and private corporation "single employer" plans controlled solely by management.

The rate of growth is equally dramatic. Less than three years ago (1980) total assets were only $650 billion; by 1994 they will exceed $3,000 billion dollars.

Pension fund assets dominate the long-term capital markets. During 1982, 65 percent of net new dollars for investment came from these funds. By the end of this decade, one-half of all capital raised for investment will come from this source. Currently, 25 percent of all stock and 40 percent of all corporate bonds are held by pension funds.

Almost all of the stock pension funds own is concentrated in the country's largest 500 corporations. Pension funds have tremendous potential over corporate management through the voting rights attached to stock ownership. Up to now they have tended to vote with corporate management on stock-holder issues.

State and local pension fund bonds are legally controlled by public officials and their appointees. However, they often turn over investment authority to banks or insurance companies. Investment decisions often cause capital to move from one sector or region of the economy to another with often dire consequences for some communities. Worker savings (including taxpayer contributions), which were once deposited in local savings institutions and invested in local housing and small businesses, are now invested in national and global capital markets.

Traditional investment practices have produced earnings below broad market averages refecting a failure of fund managers and trustees to develop a balanced investment portfolio.

THE PROBLEM

Pension funds, which depend for their health on a strong economy, have a self-interest in promoting jobs and economic development in their state. Strategic investments of pension capital in affordable housing, small business, industrial plant and equipment, and other economic activity can result in a net increase in jobs, higher tax collections and fewer individuals on public assistance.

Public employee and private pension funds are the largest capital resource available in any state. The challenge is to match this resource with states' capital needs. Sound targeted pension investments can also produce higher earnings for the retirement fund and thus ease budgetary problems. Increased earnings by the pension fund can also place the system on sounder financial footing, reducing taxpayer contributions to meet both current and future obligations to public employees and retirees.

Most public pension funds are governed by legislation specifiying how they can be invested. These statutory restrictions strongly favor investment in the stocks and bonds of the largest corporations. The restrictions sometimes state what portion of the total portfolio is to be invested in stocks and what portion in bonds. Some public funds are restricted from investment in real estate altogether. Where this is the case, development investing will have to wait on changes in the legislation.

The composition of the trustee body charged with fiduciary responsibility for the pension fund greatly influences investment policy. Some pension funds exclude members or beneficiaries from representation on the board of trustees, thus allowing members no say whatsoever in investment or fund management decisions. Some pension funds are managed entirely by bank trust departments. Alteration of the trustees' authority or composition of the board of trustees requires legislative changes.

Private pension fund trustees have long argued that they can produce the best returns when they have complete freedom to invest. More and more data are challenging that assertion. Throughout the 1970s, in fact, investment in mortgages for members would have produced a better return for pension funds than their investments in stocks and bonds -- while also providing immediate benefit to plan members and at no greater risk.

In a nutshell: strategic investing -- investing with regard for the interests of beneficiaries and of the state and local economy -- can offer financial returns equal to or greater than traditional pension fund investment policy. Development investing, however, is opposed by many fund managers and by many pension plan trustees.

The traditional investment approach has produced poor investment performance. The average earnings of pension fund investments in corporate equities from 1970-1979 was 3.9 percent. During the same decade, the stock market as a whole returned 5.9 percent. Pension funds have consistently performed below these broad market averages, earning often even less than would have been possible from passbook savings accounts. In addition, most pension funds have shown an aversion to real estate, particularly residential mortgages.

The trustees of pension funds have an important responsibility: the responsibility of guaranteeing the safety of retirement funds for hundreds or thousands of workers is an awesome one. The Employee Retirement Income Security Act (ERISA) of 1974, the federal legislation regulating private pension funds, charges trustees with maximizing the return of their funds consistent with the "prudent expert" rule (i.e. investments must be those which would be made by a prudent person acting in a like capacity). Department of Labor interpretations of ERISA have encouraged trustees to pursue conservative investment strategies.

Many trustees feel that investments targeted to job creation, local economic development, housing or mortgages for members present unacceptable levels of risk for a pension fund. The lack of a long track record for alternative investments by pension funds further increases the risk factor, some fund managers believe.

Everyone active in the pension fund arena -- plan members and beneficiaries, unions, trustees, advisors -- agree that prudence has to be the basis of all investment decisions so that retirement income can be secure. The financial integrity of a retirement system must be the cardinal concern of any pension investment policy.

Union officials have often taken the lead in promoting new approaches. Labor unions have withdrawn funds from anti-labor and non-union companies and they use the threat of divestiture to help with organizing campaigns. They also use their investments to bring pressure on corporations which close factories without adequate notice or consideration for the effect on local economies.

WHAT STATES CAN DO

Create a Pension Investment Task Force

° States should create a Pension Investment Task Force composed
  of public officials, union leaders, financial professionals,
  housing and economic development experts, and community
  groups that would: 1) conduct a complete review of the
  management and investment policies of the pension fund and
  recommend changes if necessary; 2) recommend development
  investing strategies proven successful elsewhere; 3) recommend
  changes in laws which frustrate or restrict development
  investing; and 4) educate pension fund managers and trustees,
  public officials and others, and organize constituencies in
  support of proposed changes.

Promote Pension Fund Investment in Affordable Housing, Small
Business and Jobs

° States should encourage pension funds to invest in affordable housing for pension fund beneficiaries and for moderate
  income households. Initial investments should be in residential mortgages, preferably rated pass-through securities,
  followed by investments in multi-family housing.

° States should encourage pension funds to invest in small
  business. The federally guaranteed portion of SBA loans is
  an excellent way for a pension fund to invest in small business.

° States should encourage pension funds to invest some portion
  of assets in smaller high technology corporations.

Create Regional and Municipal Development Funds

° States should urge their pension funds to participate in
  cooperative investment associations which bring together
  county, municipal and private funds for coordinated economic
  strategies.

° States should encourage their pension funds to join with
  adjacent states to create regional development banks.
  Public pension funds, private funds and other sources of
  capital would pool a portion of assets to finance larger
  scale regional projects.

Promote Responsible Investing

° States should direct pension funds to consider "social
  responsibility" investment criteria including a firm's fair
  labor practices, affirmative action, environmental protection
  and product quality record in deciding whether to invest or not.

FOR FURTHER INFORMATION

Publications

Alternative Investing by State and Local Pension Funds: Survey of Current Practices, John Petersen and Catharine Spain, Government Finance Research Center, Municipal Finance Officers' Association, 1980.

Annual Report of Pension Investment Unit, State of California, December 1982. Available from General Services, State of California, Publications Section, P.O. Box 1015, North Highlands, CA 95660.

A Model Agenda for State and Local Governments: Public Pension Fund Investment, William Schweke, 1982. $3.50. Available from the Conference on Alternative State and Local Policies.

The North Will Rise Again: Pensions, Politics and Power in the 1980s, Randy Barber and Jeremy Rifkin, Beacon Press paperback, 1978. The most influential book on this issue to date.

Pension Funds and Economic Renewal, Lawrence Litvak, Council of State Planning Agencies, 1981. $14.95. Available from the Conference on Alternative State and Local Policies.

Studies in Pension Fund Investment, Conference on Alternative State and Local Policies, 2000 Florida Avenue, N.W., Washington, D.C., 20009. A 13 book series on innovative pension fund policy and state and local experiences with alternative pension fund investment.

Organizations

CONFERENCE ON ALTERNATIVE STATE AND LOCAL POLICIES, 2000 Florida Avenue, N.W., Washington, D.C. 20009 (202) 387-6030. Has published a 13 volume series of books on innovative pension fund investing.

INVESTOR RESPONSIBILITY RESEARCH CENTER, 1319 F Street, N.W., Washington, D.C. (202) 803-3728. An information service for investors on stockholder resolutions presented to corporations.

PEOPLES BUSINESS COMMISSION, 1346 Connecticut Avenue, N.W., Washington, D.C., 20009 (202) 466-2823, Randy Barber.

PUBLIC PENSION INVESTMENT PROJECT, 240 Golden Gate Avenue, San Francisco, CA 94102. Contact: Tom Leatherwood.

Prepared by Thomas O. Leatherwood.

Plant Closings

Plant closings are a fact of life in every community and every state. Between 1978 and 1982, an estimated 12.7 million jobs disappeared nationwide -- 30 percent of existing jobs in 1978 had vanished four years later. The Northeast and Midwest alone lost approximately 900,000 jobs from 1970 to 1980.

A weak economy along with a series of major economic transformations will entail more plant closings and major layoffs. The shift from an insular national economy to an international one, from an industrial to a more information-based economy, and from cheap energy resources to more expensive ones insure that plant closings will continue to be a serious problem.

The heavily industrialized areas of the Northeast and Midwest have suffered most from plant closures. From 1969 to 1976, corporations in the "Frostbelt" states (Connecticut, Massachusetts, Michigan, Minnesota, Missouri, New York, Pennsylvania and Ohio) eliminated 111 jobs through plant shut-downs for every 100 new jobs they created. Business Week noted in 1976 that "Capital from the Northeast and Midwest has financed the industrial expansion of the South."

But southern states have also felt the impact of plant closures -- in fact, the rate of manufacturing plant closures is higher in the South than in any other region of the country.

Plant closings are now hitting such previously untouched areas as California and the Pacific Northwest states.

Where are the corporations going? To a great extent, overseas -- where labor costs are often lower. American corporate overseas investment rose tenfold from an estimated $11.8 billion in 1950 to $118.6 billion in 1974.

Plant closings oftentimes have terrible consequences. A Northeastern manufacturer may, over time, close down several facilities and shift operations to Taiwan, throwing thousands of employees out of work. When a company closes a factory, businesses servicing the employees are forced to cut back, aggravating area unemployment. Unemployed workers may spend months or years finding new jobs -- if they find work at all.

At worst, plant closings wreak havoc on individual lives, such as when eight former workers at the Federal Mogul Plant in Detroit committed suicide following the plant's closing.

THE PROBLEM

When a plant shuts down, it creates a chain of problems for the laid-off workers, local communities and the state governments. Plant closings hit older, industrial workers the hardest. They have the greatest difficulty starting their careers over again. These workers may spend months or years searching for new jobs and their unemployment benefits can run out long before they find work. A single unemployed auto worker costs the state and federal government an estimated $15,000 in transfer payments and lost taxes, according to a 1980 U. S. Department of Transportation study.

The ripple effects of plant closings on local communities and states are equally devastating. These effects include: shattered tax bases; strains on government resources as many of the unemployed are forced to seek public assistance; lost revenues to local businesses as residents' purchasing power shrinks; and what one observer calls "an industrial 'refugee' crisis of substantial magnitude--whole communities without jobs."

Plant closings are caused by "capital flight." Capital flight does not always mean the actual shutting down of a plant and moving it elsewhere. It can also mean: 1) gradually shifting equipment, employees or corporate activities from one location to another -- keeping the original facility operating but at less capacity; 2) letting older facilities run down and investing the savings elsewhere; 3) "milking" older facilities -- that is, using profits from them to bolster other corporate activities.

Maine, Michigan and Wisconsin have laws regulating plant closings. In Maine, companies with 100 or more employees which intend to shut down operations must give employees with three or more years of service one week of severance pay for each year of employment. The law provides for civil damages for noncompliance.

Michigan recently enacted the first state law for financing employee ownership, including buyouts of closing plants. Michigan's newly-created Economic Development Authority is required to finance at least five industrial conversion projects each year.

Wisconsin is the only state requiring companies to give notice (60 days) of impending shutdowns. Failure to give such notice can lead to fines of up to $50 per affected employee.

More than 20 other states are currently considering plant closing legislation. Passage will be difficult however, because of intense business lobbying.

A complete plant closings legislative program would include the following parts: (1) monitor closings and layoffs -- develop an early warning system and track national, state and local data sources; (2) provide financial assistance -- target federal funds and relevant state monies; (3) provide technical assistance on how to respond to closings and layoffs -- to workers, businesses and organized labor; (4) modify or create programs to better use existing resources -- unemployment insurance, health insurance, mortgage/rent assistance and commuting worker programs.

Although corporations strongly oppose state governments' considerations of legislation to control plant closings, many of these same corporations operate successfully in countries such as Great Britain and West Germany, which have strict plant closure laws.

Plant closing laws do not keep businesses from locating in a state. For example, United Technologies Corporation, the parent company of Pratt and Whitney Aircraft, testified against a Connecticut plant closings bill, warning it would never expand its business operations in the state if the legislation were passed. Yet a few months later, Pratt and Whitney, after looking into more than 30 possible locations in the eastern U.S. for a new plant, set up shop in Maine, the only eastern state with a plant closings law and the means for enforcing it.

The argument that expansion of service employment more than compensates for the jobs lost from plant closings and therefore, that plant closings are really not a serious problem, ignores both the nature of the service economy and the problems of those workers trained in manufacturing. Non-manufacturing jobs are frequently low-paying, part-time and usually filled by young people with special training, not middle-aged displaced factory workers. An auto assembly line worker with ten years seniority will have great difficulty becoming a computer programmer, especially when no job retraining is available.

WHAT STATES CAN DO

Prenotification

° States should pass legislation requiring one year advance
notice of intent to close or relocate a company or displace
over 15 percent of the firm's employees. Prenotification is
essential to give government and workers the time to prepare
for shutdowns or enable them to try to keep the plant
operating.

To Assist Workers

° States should create an Economic Adjustment Task Force to
retrain workers, place them in new jobs and modernize
business facilities.

° States should set up programs to help jobless workers commute
from communities hit by plant closures and mass layoffs
to other communities. California is currently designing a
program to match the skills of Salinas/Monterey area workers
with job opportunities in the San Jose/Santa Clara area.

° States should instruct all public lenders, such as state
housing finance agencies and veteran loan programs, to
restructure payment arrangments for persons unemployed as
a result of plant closings.

° States should provide health insurance benefits to unemployed
and disabled individuals who are eligible for unemployment
compensation payments.

Employee Buyouts

° States should create development banks that can finance
employee buyouts. States could require recipients of the
aid to set aside a minimum percentage of stock to be
employee-owned. The Massachusetts Community Development
Finance Corporation, for example, can make debt or equity
investments in worker-owned businesses.

Severance Payments

° States should require the company to pay a sum equal to 15
percent of the total annual payroll of its plants into a
Community Assistance Fund. Such a fund would be used to
preserve current jobs, to attract new industry into the
community or to maintain the existing tax base, if the
company closes down any of its plants.

° States should pass legislation requiring the firm closing
down a plant to make severance payments to the terminated
employees equal to one week's pay for each year worked.

FOR FURTHER INFORMATION

Publications

Corporate Flight, Barry Bluestone, Bennett Harrison and Lawrence Baker, 1981. Available for $3.95 from the Conference on Alternative State and Local Policies. A thorough examination of the causes, consequences and responses to plant closings.

Planning Guidebook for Communities Facing a Plant Closing or Mass Layoff, January 1983. Free from the California Office of Planning and Policy Development, 1030 13th Street, Suite 200, Sacramento, CA 95814.

Plant Closings: Resources for Public Officials and Trade Unionists, Ed Kelly and Lee Webb, 1979. Available for $5.95 from the Conference on Alternative State and Local Policies. A compendium of articles on plant closings, including European policies, state initiatives and federal responses.

Plant Modernization and Community Economic Stability: Proceedings of a Conference, January 1983. Available for $7.00 from the Bureau of Governmental Research and Service, P.O. Box 3177, Eugene, OR 97403.

Organizations

CONFERENCE ON ALTERNATIVE STATE AND LOCAL POLICIES, 2000 Florida Ave., N.W., Washington, D.C. (202) 387-6030, Lee Webb, Director. Publishes studies on plant closings and periodic updates on new state legislation.

NATIONAL CENTER FOR EMPLOYEE OWNERSHIP, 1611 Walter Reed Drive, Room 109 Arlington, VA 22204 (703) 931-2757, Corey Rosen, Executive Director. NCEO sells a variety of publications explaining the legal, economic and organizational aspects of employee ownership.

OHIO PUBLIC INTEREST CAMPAIGN, 340 Chester, 12th Building, Cleveland, OH 44114 (216) 861-5200, Ed Kelley, Research Director. A statewide citizens group focusing on plant closings, energy and tax policy.

UNITED AUTO WORKERS, 8000 East Jefferson, Detroit, MI 48214 (313) 926-5000. Sheldon Friedman, Research Director. Friedman is a leading specialist on the issue. The UAW has done extensive research on the issue and has lobbied for state and national plant closings legislation.

Prepared by David Jones and William Schweke.

Small Business

BACKGROUND FACTS

Approximately 98 percent of all American businesses are "small." Only 10,000 of the nation's businesses have 500 or more employees. Small business employs 47 percent of the non-governmental labor force.

Almost 80 percent of all net new jobs come from firms with fewer than 100 employees, according to research done at MIT between 1969 and 1976, and two-thirds of all new jobs are accounted for by firms with 20 or fewer employees. Futhermore, in the Northeast small business job gains made up for opportunities lost by the largest corporations during the same period.

In addition, National Science Foundation and Commerce Department reports concluded that small business was "24 times more innovative per research and development dollar than large firms." Thus, contrary to popular belief, a state's job creation, even in the sunbelt states, will come from fostering local businesses, not from attracting business from out of state.

Yet for small business, lack of access to capital is a major problem, and the economic recession has severely magnified this problem. The rate of business failures in 1982 and 1983 is running five times ahead of the rate in 1981.

Venture capital is important to growing small businesses, but not as important as often assumed. In a $3 trillion economy that invests over $500 billion a year in capital, the venture capital industry accounts for approximately $1 billion a year, or one fifth of one percent. That money is invested in a few thousand of the ten to thirteen million small business concerns in the United States.

By contrast, regulated financial institutions in the United States, including banks, savings and loans, thrifts, savings banks, credit unions, insurance reserves and pension funds control over five trillion dollars a year in assets.

Commercial banks alone control over $2 trillion in assets. The average sized state has approximately $40 billion in assets in commercial banks.

THE PROBLEM

The biggest problem that small business faces is the need for capital at affordable interest rates. The lack of access to capital or access but at too high a rate of interest has a devastating impact on the survival of existing small businesses and on the chances for new small businesses to open their doors.

Capital for large and small businesses alike comes from banks, insurance companies and other financial institutions. Financial institutions are regulated at both the state and federal level, with the federal government dominating. The exception is that states regulate insurance reserves. Since the 1930s, regulatory policy has focused on assuring the safety and soundness of the institutions, with little thought given to how regulation affects the ability of these institutions to meet legitimate capital needs.

Ironically, this focus on safety and soundness -- which usually takes the form of prohibiting institutions from taking excessive risk in their investment activity -- may have contributed significantly to the economic malaise now eating away at the financial institutions themselves.

Most small businesses finance their working capital with short term, bank-financed debt. The gyrating increases in the interest rates have severely strained the debt-service capabilities of most small businesses. Without the internal reserves to withstand the long period of high rates, and without an ability to fully pass along these increased "costs" of doing business to their customers, small businesses are forced to close their doors. The farm sector, comprised mostly of small businesses, has also experienced a steep economic decline.

Over the most recent business cycle, the cost of credit (interest rates) and the variability of these rates, rather than credit availability, have been the major problem because they undermine the ability of business managers to plan, profit flows are much less predictable and the risks of undertaking new investments are greater.

Since approximately 80 percent of small businesses rely on financing from depository institutions, an increase in the cost of financing and a decrease in the availability of funds has a more severe impact on smaller firms than on larger firms.

For potentially growing businesses, the problem of capital access is severe. Options are severely limited for businesses that cannot provide security, collateral or guarantees for loans from banks whose major management and regulatory responsibility is to avoid any risk. They must then turn to personal money, family and friends, utilization of non-business assets as collateral or in rare cases, private venture capital.

The Small Business Administration's direct loan and loan guarantee programs have helped, but are being reduced. In fact, the SBA program is a very modest capital correcting mechanism that needs expansion to counter the government's capital market interference.

There is some controversy over whether capital access is the most important problem or whether the cost of capital is more important. Both are important, but some capital access problems can be solved through modest and inexpensive market restructuring, while reducing the cost of capital is largely a question of federal fiscal and monetary policy and/or expensive subsidies.

The new public policies being proposed for small businesses are basically oriented toward improving capital access, not reducing the capital cost. This will help many businesses at little or no government cost, but will not solve the problem for other businesses that require capital to survive or expand.

These program proposals should not aim exclusively to satisfy a small business constituency, but to create a climate of economic and job growth. The potential entrepreneur and the struggling, growing company -- not mature small businesses more interested in protecting their gains -- should be targeted for aid. The goal of making financial institutions more responsive to the needs of small businesses will be well received, but specific program proposals should extend beyond the interests of the organized small business political constituencies. Therefore, new public policies should be pursued as part of an overall strategy of economic growth, not as a small business constituency issue.

WHAT STATES CAN DO

Bank Regulation

° States should require financial regulators, in their annual report to the governor and legislature, to report on the performance of the institutions in supporting productive business development.

° States should develop a state-level equivalent of the 1977 federal Community Reinvestment Act, which directed regulators to consider whether banks were meeting the needs of the community. Such an act should focus on a bank's record in meeting the needs of small business as well as consumers and mortgage loans.

° States should ensure that small businesses are represented on the boards of directors of major financial institutions. Major banks seldom have small business representation.

New State Programs

° States should establish Loan Loss Reserve Programs. These programs develop a special reserve fund to allow banks to make loans of more than normal risk. They work best in states that have a substantial percentage of banking assets in large banks, since the program requires each participating bank to develop a loss reserve covering a broad portfolio of loans.

° States should create a new class of commercial lenders to provide funds for venture capital firms. California, Nevada and some other states have created "Business and Industrial Development Corporations" (BIDCOs) to generate more sophisticated financing for venture capital companies. These institutions make government guaranteed loans and sell the guarantees to leverage their funds. Since they do not take deposits and do not have fiduciary responsibility or federal insurance, they can take equity positions and develop much more flexible financing responses than is the case for banks.

Investing Pension Funds

° States should use its regulatory power to ensure that pension funds and insurance reserves are used for small business development. Investments in smaller businesses, after accounting for overhead and risk, can generate better returns than investments in larger companies.

FOR FURTHER INFORMATION

Publications

Banking and Small Business, 1981, Derek Hansen, Council of State Planning Agencies. Available from the Conference on Alternative State and Local Policies for $14.95.

Expanding the Opportunity to Produce, 1981, Robert Friedman and Bill Schweke, eds. Corporation for Enterprise Development. Collection of articles by 52 nationally prominent experts on promoting new enterprise development. Available for $19.95.

The Entrepreneurial Economy: The Monthly Review of Enterprise Development Strategies, available from the Corporation for Enterprise Development, $78/year.

Pension Funds and Economic Renewal, 1981, Lawrence Litvak, Council of State Planning Agencies. Available from the Conference on Alternative State and Local Policies, $14.95.

Small Business Policy for California, California State CETA Office, Attention: MATS Unit, 80 Capitol Mall, Mic 77, Sacramento, CA 95814.

Small Business and State Economic Development, available through the Counsel for Community Development, Inc., 10 Concord Ave., Cambridge, MA.

Organizations

CONFERENCE ON ALTERNATIVE STATE AND LOCAL POLICIES, 2000 Florida Avenue, N.W., Washington, D.C. 20009 (202) 387-6030.

CORPORATION FOR ENTERPRISE DEVELOPMENT, 1211 Connecticut Avenue, N.W., Suite 710 A, Washington, D.C. 20036 (202) 293-7963.

COUNCIL OF STATE PLANNING AGENCIES, 444 North Capitol Street, Suite 291, Washington, D.C. 20001 202-624-5386.

NATIONAL FEDERATION OF INDEPENDENT BUSINESS, L'Enfant Plaza East, S.W., Washington, D.C.

OFFICE OF POLICY DEVELOPMENT, Office of the Governor, State Capitol, Albany, NY 12224.

Prepared by Derek Hansen.

Natural Resources and Environment

Farm and Food Policy

BACKGROUND FACTS

The American food system is today in an increasingly
vulnerable position. Farmers and consumers are increasingly
threatened by powerful economic and political trends.

Farmers presently face the worst economic situation since
the Great Depression. Total farm income was $32.4 billion
in 1979. It fell sharply to $20.1 billion in 1980. It rose
a bit to $25.1 billion in 1981. It fell dramatically to
$19.5 billion in 1982. In constant 1967 dollars, 1982 farm
income was lower than in any year since 1933.

A much smaller number of farmers raise more food on
larger farms. Production is intensive, highly mechanized,
dependent on large capital outlays, very specialized by region
and on individual farms and heavily reliant on chemical fertil-
izers, pesticides, herbicides and energy.

Ownership and operation of farms are diverging, as
outside investors enter the sector and as the cost of owning
a farm rises above the means of most.

Economic clout is becoming concentrated among fewer farms.
About one-fifth of all farms now account for four-fifths of
total farm sales.

The average farm size has been increasing for decades.
In 1940 it was 175 acres; today it is over 400.

Farmers are losing control over production and marketing
of their crops and livestock. They must buy inputs from and
sell their products to dominant large corporations.

About 3 million acres of the 540-million acre cropland
are lost each year to suburban development, lakes, highways,
shopping centers and other non-farm uses.

Consumer food prices, despite recent moderation, seem
to be on a constantly rising course, while farm income is
currently at near-depression levels. On average the farmer
gets less than 40 cents of the consumer's food dollar.

Farm debt and loan delinquencies are rising. At the
beginning of 1982 over half of Farmers Home Administration
one-year farm operating loans were delinquent.

THE PROBLEM

Agriculture in the United States was once a relatively simple pursuit, as it remains in the "underdeveloped" Third World. In the past, farmers using relatively simple technologies produced food and fiber that was, for the most part, consumed locally or regionally. Today that system is radically different.

Food marketing today is also very different from the distribution system of a few decades ago. Consumers now buy fruit, vegetables, poultry and other items shipped thousands of miles as production concentrates in some areas. In addition, many farmers now export large parts of their crop.

All of this change has resulted in a food system of prodigious efficiency and productivity. We have strawberries in January, but at what cost? Beneath the successes -- and often rising above them -- are numerous flaws: unstable farm income, consumer dissatisfaction, disappearing family farms, soil erosion, farmland loss and water depletion. Agriculture also suffers from chronic economic instability. Farm debt and foreclosures are now at record levels.

The food distribution system has become fully industrialized. Now the system of production -- farming itself -- is also on the verge of industrialization. This may or may not lead to greater efficiency. The replacement of family farms by larger production units with hired workers, farm managers and absentee owners will also aggravate major problems or create new ones. For example, research shows that when family farms decline rural communities and small businesses also suffer.

For more than a hundred years government has undertaken programs and policies aimed at supporting or rescuing agriculture generally and the family farm specifically. Beginning in the 1860s, a vast array of federal programs has helped develop agriculture. Price supports, tax breaks, research, extension education, subsidized credit and marketing aids are only the most prominent efforts.

Yet in many ways the laws and regulations intended to help have instead fueled some of the most unfortunate trends in contemporary agriculture. For example, many of the programs have helped mainly owners of the larger farms or have even enticed non-farm investors and corporations into agriculture as competitors against the family farm. Another facet is that black farmers are fast disappearing.

Further complicating this picture are the Reagan administration's budget cuts in domestic programs. The few agricultural programs of real benefit to small farm operators or consumers are being cut back or face the threat of cuts, while the few new programs will go mostly to large-scale operators. An example is the payment-in-kind grain giveaway to farmers in exchange for keeping land out of production.

State governments have a responsibility to fill at least some of the breach. Some states have adopted one or more pieces of a progressive agenda for agriculture and many excellent ideas are under consideration.

° For example, to limit loss of cropland to development, Oregon requires that local governments have exclusive farm use zoning plans.

° In West Virginia there is a state-run system of farmers' markets in major cities.

° Eight states restrict non-family farm corporate ownership of farmland.

° Missouri and Texas have small farm extension programs which specifically reach out to help limited-resource operators.

° Minnesota has a law which expands the authority of state courts to grant injunctive relief to farmers threatened by foreclosures. The courts may grant a moratorium of up to one year and restructure the loan payments. Several other states have adopted or are considering measures on foreclosures.

Many of those who approve of current trends in agriculture believe that bigger is better, that growth in farm size is necessary and inevitable. They believe there are too many people in farming and that chemicals are essential to high productivity.

While it is true that many very small farms cannot achieve economic viability through agriculture alone, farms do not have to be enormous to achieve maximum economies of size. For example, research by the U.S. Department of Agriculture shows that in 1979 full efficiency was achieved on a grain farm with annual sales of $133,000 and size of 314 acres. Growth beyond that size adds to sales and profits, but not to increased efficiency.

Chemicals have greatly increased yields over the last several decades. But they have also become very expensive, caused environmental deterioration, depleted the soil, led to poison-resistant pests and created other problems. A mixed use of chemical -- that is, "conventional" -- and organic products would be a much better practice.

WHAT STATES CAN DO

Preservation of Agricultural Land

° States should adopt comprehensive, integrated plans to keep
  productive land in farming. Plans could include exclusive
  agricultural zoning, tax incentives for farmland retention
  and public purchase of land development rights.

Economic and Credit Assistance

° States should provide financial assistance to the economically beleaguered farmer. State farm lending programs
  could supplement federal aid. Some taxes on agriculture
  might be forgiven. And land banks could be formed to buy
  land from those who must sell. States should also provide
  help to farmers threatened by mortgage foreclosures. The
  Minnesota law noted above is an excellent model.

° States should establish programs to provide credit at reasonable terms to low-equity and beginning farmers. Ten states
  now have such programs. Included in programs should be (1)
  a partial interest subsidy; and (2) a requirement that
  borrowers have both farming skills and a net worth below
  some reasonable ceiling.

Marketing

° States should begin or improve direct marketing programs.
  Existing markets, parking lots, shopping centers and other
  facilities could be used as market sites, so that local
  farmers can bring crops for direct sale to consumers.

° States should require hospitals, schools and other public
  institutions to give preference to supplies of locally-grown
  food.

Research and Extension

° States should refocus their research and extension systems
  toward the needs of small and moderate sized farms.

° States also should require that their research and extension
  systems to investigate the use of organic agriculture.

The Structure of Farming

° States should place limits on non-family farm corporate and
  absentee ownership of agricultural assets. Family farm corporations should be exempt from any such limits. Foreign
  ownership of farmland should be monitored and if necessary,
  controlled.

FOR FURTHER INFORMATION

Publications

Assisting Beginning Farmers: New Programs and Responses, 1980, Conference on Alternative State and Local Policies, $3.95.

Empty Breadbasket: The Coming Challenge to America's Food Supply, 1981, Cornucopia Project of Rodale Press, $5.00.

New Directions in Farm, Land and Food Policy: A Time for State and Local Action, 1979, Conference on Alternative State and Local Policies, $4.95.

New Initiatives in Farm, Land and Food Legislation: A State-by-State Guide, 1981, Conference on Alternative State and Local Policies, $3.95.

Protecting Farmland: A Guidebook for State and Local Governments, 1981. Available from USDA, SCS, 6117 South Building, Washington, D.C. 20250. (202) 447-7443.

Organizations

CENTER FOR RURAL AFFAIRS, P.O. Box 405, Walthill, NE 68067 (402) 846-5428.

CONFERENCE ON ALTERNATIVE STATE AND LOCAL POLICIES, 2000 Florida Avenue, N.W., Washington, D.C. 20009 (202) 387-6030. Extensive publications on family farm issues and farmland preservation.

CORNUCOPIA PROJECT OF RODALE PRESS, 33 East Minor Street, Emmaus, PA 18049 (215) 967-5171. Information on local and regional self-sufficient food systems.

NATIONAL ASSOCIATION OF STATE DEPARTMENTS OF AGRICULTURE, 1616 H Street, N.W., Washington, D.C. 20006 (202) 628-1566. The Farmland Preservation Project does research on successful farmland preservation programs and publishes a free monthly newsletter, Farmland Notes.

NATIONAL FARMERS ORGANIZATION, 485 L'Enfant Plaza, S.W., Washington, D.C. 20004 (202) 484-7075. General farm organization.

NATIONAL FARMERS UNION, 12025 East 45th Avenue, Denver, CO 80251 (303) 371-1760. General farm organization with affiliates in many states.

RURAL AMERICA, 1900 M Street, N.W., Washington, D.C. 20036 (202) 659-2800. David Raphael, Executive Director.

Prepared by Joe Belden.

Environmental Protection

BACKGROUND FACTS

An April 1983 New York Times/CBS News poll found that 58 percent of Americans agreed that protecting the environment is so important that requirements and standards cannot be too high, and continuing environmental improvements must be made regardless of cost.

A March 1982 Harris poll found that 80 percent of Republicans, 85 percent of Democrats, and 84 percent of independents favored stricter enforcement of air and water pollution standards.

A June 1981 Newsweek magazine poll found found that 75 percent of Americans believe it is possible to maintain strong economic growth and high environmental standards. A September 1981 New York Times/CBS poll found that two-thirds of its respondents favored keeping strict air pollution laws even if some factories had to close.

These poll results demonstrate a widespread public belief that pollution and misuse of natural resources pose serious threats to personal health and welfare.

The Reagan administration's efforts to cut back every federal environmental program have been stalled in Congress. The resignations in disgrace of EPA chief Anne Burford and Rita Lavelle have even forced the White House to recognize the importance of the environment as a political issue. The appointment of William Ruckelshaus to be administrator of EPA changes the symbol, but doesn't guarantee a major change in administration policy on environmental issues.

Environmental legislation in the 1970s has improved the health and well-being of Americans. Between 1970 and 1980, for instance, sulfur content of air dropped by 17 percent, although scientists in 1970 had estimated that sulfur content would rise by 50 percent.

Citizen involvement has rapidly increased in environmental PACs, labor and environmental coalitions, and grassroots efforts such as acid rain monitoring networks and recycling centers. These activities build a strong base to defend federal environmental laws and supplement them with strong local and state programs.

THE PROBLEM

Americans have been concerned for many years with keeping air and water clean and preserving wilderness areas. The serious environmental problems of the 1980s are bringing those concerns even closer to home.

Toxic waste contamination and radiation incidents at dumpsites and reactors, such as at Love Canal and Three Mile Island, have made "backyard" issues out of the environmental problems.

At the same time, significant progress has been achieved in cleaning up traditional sources of air and water pollution. This progress has demonstrated our ability to solve pollution problems without staggering economic consequences. This progress has created new support for environmental programs and it has created new pollution control industries that benefit from environmental programs.

The Reagan administration has assaulted, across the board, environmental and resources management programs. Their environmental policies were exposed publicly through the controversies and resignations of Anne Burford and Rita Lavelle. This attention has led to the appointment of William Ruckelshaus to head the EPA. His appointment is an indication of political concern, but not necessarily a sign of change in administration environmental policies. Indeed, the initial Ruckelshaus positions on Clean Water Act revisions and the EPA budget show little if any improvement in administration attitudes.

In tandem with the Reagan policies, the explosive growth of business political action committees and industrial "job blackmail" has brought environmental issues into the partisan political arena.

Contributions from polluting industries to political candidates clearly have influenced Congress. In many communities bad economic conditions have given corporations a great opportunity to use the threat of cutting jobs to beat back needed environmental regulation.

The response to these threats has been unprecedented. Citizen organizing on environmental issues has grown dramatically. Environmental political action committees donate money and volunteers to worthy national and state candidates across the country to offset the influence of polluter PACs. New citizen networks monitor the acidity of rainfall and the impact of acid rain on local lakes and streams.

States play a crucial role in land use and resource conservation. The Reagan administration has halted virtually all parkland acquisition, yet many irreplaceable resources are threatened by industrial or mining development and suburban sprawl.

Free flowing rivers, prime farmlands and urban open spaces can often be most effectively protected by local and state programs that work with local landowners and community leaders. Minnesota's wild and scenic rivers system is an example of a successful local resources protection program, using a mix of acquisition, regulation and "less than fee" purchases to manage scenic state rivers.

Because of the retreat in federal programs, state environmental programs are more crucial than ever. James Watt and other administration officials call for the return of environmental programs to the states, but refuse to provide the resources to enforce those programs in the states. State leaders must speak out both in support of important federal programs and to provide adequate funding for state environmental programs.

Strong state enforcement of mine safety and workplace health regulation must also replace federal programs crippled by Secretary Watt and OSHA Administrator Thorne Auchter.

State officials must also guard against federal preemption of stricter state pollution control rules in the name of regulatory reform. For example, attempts have been made in Congress to prevent California from enforcing stricter clean air provisions and other states from adopting strict pesticide regulations.

Labor unions and environmentalists are working together to secure a healthy workplace and community, together with economic stability and prosperity. The OSHA/Environmental Network in particular is a nationwide coalition of labor unions and environmental organizations that work on the federal Clean Air Act and OSHA regulations. In many states, the Network has worked on "community right to know" laws and toxic chemical programs. Together, these groups accuratly assess the real economic costs of regulation and can reveal the often spurious nature of alleged links between environmental regulations and plant closures.

WHAT STATES CAN DO

Enforcing Anti-Pollution Laws

° States should increase funding and staffing for the enforcement and administration of their pollution control programs.
The increases are needed to compensate for federal budget
cutbacks that leave EPA enforcement activities understaffed
and underfunded.

Developing Local Energy Security

° States should enact legislation to encourage utility investment in conservation. Utilities should make loans for
insulation, weatherization and solar hot water. In addition,
to the energy savings, local businesses and workers will get
additional profits and jobs.

° States should enact heavy truck weight distance taxes
rather than increase regressive gasoline taxes. Trucks are
responsible for most highway damage according to recent
federal and state studies.

° States should establish an integrated bicycle transportation
program that provides safe access to major areas of employment and secure weatherprotected storage for bicycles.

Conserving Our Resources

° States should establish wild and scenic river programs to
protect them for public use. States should acquire critical
habitats and undeveloped tracts for parks in urbanizing
areas. Where outright acquisition is impossible, environ-
mentally sensitive lands can be protected through regional
zoning efforts.

° States should establish soil conservation and organic farm
research programs to stop losses of topsoil and encourage
alternatives to the current inefficient agricultural practices.

° States should enact bottle and can deposit laws. Such laws
have proven effective in nine states. New York recently
became the tenth state.

° States should create state conservation corps that hire
unemployed youths to work rehabilitating urban parks and state
parks and forests. California has a very successful program.

° States should establish programs to stimulate reforestation
and wise use of existing forest resources. California
provides saplings to rural landowners and a small hourly wage
to plant them on their property.

FOR FURTHER INFORMATION

Publications

Fear At Work: Job Blackmail, Labor and the Environment,
by Richard Kazis and Richard Grossman, Environmentalists for
Full Employment, 1536 16th St., N.W., Washington, D.C. 20036,
$9.95. An expose of corporate campaigns to weaken workplace
and environmental regulations by using the promise of jobs
and the threat of unemployment.

The Green Vote Handbook, Sierra Club, 530 Bush Street,
San Francisco, CA 94108. A useful introduction to politics
for environmentalists.

Progress as if Survival Mattered, edited by Hugh Nash,
Friends of the Earth Books, 1045 Sansome St., San Francisco,
CA 94111, $14.95. A major compendium of articles on environ-
mental problems and opportunites.

Ronald Reagan and the American Environment, Friends of
the Earth Books, 1045 Sansome St., San Francisco, CA 94111,
$6.95. A critique by ten national environmental groups of
Reagan's environmental policies.

Organizations

ENVIRONMENTAL ACTION, 1346 Connecticut Ave., N.W., Suite 731,
Washington, D.C. 20036 (202) 833-1845. Runs a national
clearinghouse on bottle bill legislation in states and cities.

FRIENDS OF THE EARTH, 530 7th Street, S.E., Washington, D.C.,
20003 (202) 543-4312. Peter Lafen, Transportation Counsel.
An environmental group working on a wide range of issues.

LEAGUE OF AMERICAN WHEELMEN, 112 South 16th Street, Philadelphia,
PA 19102 (215) 564-0855. Ralph Hirsch, Legislative Director.
National organization of bicycle activists.

LEAGUE OF CONSERVATION VOTERS, 317 Pennsylvania Avenue, S.E.
Washington, D.C., 20003 (202) 547-7200. Marion Edey, Director.
The largest environmental political action committee.

THE OSHA/ENVIRONMENT NETWORK, 815 16th Street, N.W., Room 301,
Washington, D.C., 20006, (202) 842-7820. Pam Woywod, Director.
A national network of worker health and community safety
organizations.

Prepared by Peter M. Lafen.

Nuclear Energy

<u>BACKGROUND FACTS</u>

Nuclear power would pose little or no risk, according to its earliest advocates. And the electricity it produced would be "too cheap to meter."

Thirty years later, that optimism appears as a parody of reality. The amount of highly radioactive nuclear waste grows constantly with no solution in sight; profoundly serious issues have arisen concerning the safety of nuclear power; and utilities are nearly bankrupt in many areas of the country because they committed themselves to nuclear reactors.

The bright future of nuclear power began to dim in the mid-1970s. Costs escalated rapidly, to the point that prominent analysts argued that even coal-fired plants, with their high fuel costs, were more economical than nuclear power. By the early 1980s, nuclear plants predicted to cost $900 million or less had risen in cost to $4 billion, with no maximum in sight.

More important than costs, however, were safety concerns. In 1975, a serious fire occurred at the Browns Ferry facility in Alabama. In 1976, a Nuclear Regulatory Commission (NRC) staff member with broad responsibilities over several reactors, and three members of the General Electric nuclear program resigned in protest over inadequate safety precautions. In 1979, an accident occurred at Unit 2 of the Three Mile Island facility in Pennsylvania. Tens of thousands of people evacuated the area.

Three Mile Island might have been a turning point, spurring stricter safety measures and greater protection. Instead, there was a backlash that ultimately resulted in intense pressures to grant reactor licenses without delay and the important safety lessons of the accident have been largely ignored.

While public attention has focused on the reactor safety issue, the long-term problem of nuclear waste remains unresolved despite recent Congressional enactment of the Nuclear Waste Policy Act of 1982. The Act establishes ambitious schedules for development of waste storage and disposal facilities, but it has not solved the technical and socio-political problems that have always plagued the waste issue.

THE PROBLEM

The use of nuclear reactors poses three fundamental problems: reactor safety, radioactive waste management and disposal, and grossly excessive cost. Until recently, the role of the states in any of these issues has been severely limited, partly by federal preemption and partly by the failure of state utility regulatory commissions to require sound financial planning by nuclear utilities.

Reactor safety is clearly beyond the bounds of state authority in terms of technical requirements. Under the Atomic Energy Act the Nuclear Regulatory Commission has complete authority in that area. However, states have an important role in emergency planning for possible reactor accidents.

State activity with respect to radioactive waste management and disposal has recently been formalized by the Nuclear Waste Policy Act of 1982. The Act establishes procedures for state involvement in waste disposal decisions, including possible state veto of a disposal site within its boundaries. The Act also includes provisions for federal reimbursement of some costs of state participation.

Ultimately the problem of nuclear energy is the problem of how best to meet the nation's energy needs in both the short and the long term. It is here that cost becomes extremely important and here is where states can take the lead. The massive amounts of capital committed to nuclear power stretched utilities to the breaking point. They have also diverted essential resources from the development of less costly, less capital-intensive, more efficient and safer means of providing energy.

State Responses   Efforts in Congress and elsewhere at the federal level to bring rationality to the nuclear issue have been thwarted by the Reagan administration's abdication of energy policy and by the nuclear industry's political influence in Congress.

The states have been far more creative and sensitive to the serious problems of nuclear power, but to date they have been frustrated by federal preemption. Fortunately, a recent Supreme Court decision has emphatically confirmed state authority to address many issues that relate to nuclear power. On April 20, 1983, the Supreme Court upheld California laws that ban new nuclear reactors until a solution has been found for the disposal of nuclear wastes (Pacific Gas & Electric Co. v. State Energy Resources Conservation and Development Commission, Docket No. 81-1945 filed April 20, 1983). The principles established in the decision go far beyond the particular action taken by California, to the point that Justices Blackmun and Stevens in a concurring opinion argued that a state may ban nuclear power plants simply out of fear of meltdown or other nuclear catastrophe. Other states have already followed California's lead on the nuclear waste issue, and they should explore other means by which to regulate or limit nuclear power.

A major tool of state action should be the state regulatory commission, which often has the authority to regulate expenditures by state utilities, thereby controlling the size and type of generating plants. A strong state commission can prevent unwise investment in a nuclear facility.

Similarly, those states that refuse to grant rate increases to pay for Construction Work in Progress (CWIP) force the utilities to use their own money to fund nuclear construction. Since nuclear plants are generally perceived as bad investments, this should effectively halt nuclear construction in a state where it occurs. However, this sort of action is threatened by the federal Energy Regulatory Commission, which has recently voted to permit CWIP for all states under its jurisdiction.

Another area where serious state action should be fruitful is emergency planning. All nuclear reactors are required to have emergency plans that provide for protection, including evacuation, up to at least 10 miles from the reactors. In many cases, such planning has been nothing more than a sham, with no real assurances that traffic estimates and evacuation times are reasonably correct. States should insist on the use of independent consultants with no ties to the nuclear industry and demand that the needs and interests of localities be addressed in full.

State programs to conserve energy, manage peak loads, encourage conservation and promote alternative energy sources will probably have more impact than any other policies in minimizing the use of nuclear power. With no real need, nuclear reactors cannot be justified on economic grounds.

In fact, nuclear energy provides a relatively small percentage (11 percent) of only one type of energy -- electricity -- which constitutes a relatively small proportion of our total energy use. Since only about 9 percent of U.S. electricity is generated with oil, even complete replacement of that amount with nuclear power would have little effect. All of America's nuclear reactors could be replaced by a major conservation effort conducted in conjunction with intensive development of alternative energy sources.

Finally, some state attempts to regulate the transportation of nuclear wastes have withstood challenge. See City of New York v. U.S. Department of Transportation, 539 F. Supp. 1237 (S.D.N.Y. 1982).

WHAT STATES CAN DO

Nuclear Waste

° States should carefully review the Supreme Court decision on California's waste legislation and shape their own legislative efforts to comply with the standards adopted by the Court.

° States should participate to the fullest extent in the mechanisms established by the Nuclear Waste Policy Act of 1982, particularly if they are potential sites for waste repositories.

° All states through which radioactive wastes may be transported should enact restrictions to regulate that transportation.

Controlling the Generation Mix and Minimizing Costs

° States should require the use of independent consultants to evaluate utility projections and to develop independent cost and need projections. These consultants can be paid through levies against the utilities.

° States should pass legislation banning the use of Construction Work in Progress (CWIP) payments.

° States should establish and require utilities to establish programs to promote energy conservation, load management, cogeneration and the use of alternative energy sources.

° States should clearly establish that unneeded plants will not be allowed in the utilities' rate bases.

Nuclear Safety

° States should be closely involved in the emergency planning process for reactors within their borders or near their borders and should demand independent consultants and accurate and realistic assumptions.

° States should participate in licensing hearings and should provide substantial resources to evaluate and refute the positions taken by the utilities and the NRC staff.

° States should establish special offices to represent the public or should require utilities to contribute to a special fund to pay for participation by citizen groups in NRC licensing hearings and in state rate and other regulatory proceedings.

FOR FURTHER INFORMATION

Publications

    Accidents Will Happen: The Case Against Nuclear Power,
Lee Stephenson and George R. Zachar, Eds., The Environmental
Action Foundation, Harper & Row, 1979. Useful introductory
material on the full range of nuclear issues.

    The Cult of the Atom, Daniel F. Ford, Simon and Schuster,
1982. A comprehensive history of the regulation of nuclear
power.

    The Next Nuclear Gamble: Transportation and Storage of
Nuclear Waste, Marvin Resnikoff, Council on Economic Priorities,
New York, 1983. The most recent work on nuclear waste issues.

    Power Plant Cost Escalation: Nuclear and Coal Capital
Costs, and Economics, Charles Komanoff, Komanoff Energy
Associates, New York, 1981. The best information available
on the costs of nuclear construction.

Organizations

CRITICAL MASS ENERGY PROJECT, 215 Pennsylvania Avenue, S.E.,
Washington, D.C. 20003 (202) 546-4996. An organization
concerned with all aspects of nuclear issues.

ENVIRONMENTAL ACTION and ENVIRONMENTAL ACTION FOUNDATION,
1346 Conn. Ave., N.W., Washington, D.C. 20036 (202) 833-1845
and 659-1130. Closely related organizations with information
on all issues and particular strengths in the areas of costs
and rate impacts of nuclear power and alternative energy sources.

NUCLEAR INFORMATION AND RESOURCE SERVICE, 1346 Connecticut
Avenue, N.W., Washington, D.C. 20036 (202) 296-7552. A
clearinghouse for nuclear information.

UNION OF CONCERNED SCIENTISTS, 1346 Connecticut Avenue,
N.W., Washington, D.C. 20036 (202) 296-5600. A technically-
oriented organization with knowledge of all areas and particular
expertise in nuclear safety issues.

Prepared by William Jordan.

Energy Conservation

Two nationwide polls in the 1980 Presidential campaign discovered that more Americans want to use renewable energy to meet energy demand than any other energy strategy.

This popular support should come as no surprise. Used wisely, power from the sun, wind, falling water and organic plants is gentle to the environment. Such power is cheaper -- and poses fewer safety risks -- than fossil fuel or nuclear energy.

After two major oil price increases, energy conservation has also become a widely used and accepted strategy of American energy planning. American buildings, industries and vehicles are 18 percent more efficient today than they were in 1973.

Still tiny by fossil energy industry standards, the solar and conservation industries have nevertheless grown dramatically in the past four years. For example, the number of passive solar homes, in which the building itself functions as a solar collector, increased from approximately 500 in 1977 to almost 80,000 in 1982. National alcohol fuel capacity increased from 1.5 million gallons in 1978 to 400 million gallons in 1982.

In 1980, sales for active solar systems, passive solar designs, photovoltaics, wind energy machines, biomass conversion, hydroelectric facilities and geothermal systems reached $4.5 billion.

U.S. spending for energy conservation rose from less than $2 billion in 1978, and is expected to reach $8.7 billion in 1985 and $50 billion in 1990, according to Business Week.

A variety of government and university studies confirm that conservation and solar measures are our nation's wisest and most economic energy alternatives. According to A New Prosperity, the U.S. can increase productivity and reduce energy needs by 25 percent simply by increasing the efficiency of energy use.

THE PROBLEM

Energy is a major problem for the United States, although a temporary oil surplus has slightly reduced energy prices. Despite reduced oil imports, the U.S. still spends scores of billions for foreign oil. The resulting poor balance-of-payments and inflation have been key sources of our economic problems. Moreover, this country's oil supply lines from the Middle East remain militarily vulnerable.

From an environmental perspective our conventional power plants continue to produce acid rain, carbon dioxide and radioactive wastes. Some new energy plans call for increased stripping of the land for coal production and diversion of the West's precious water resources.

Unfortunately, the Reagan administration has developed a dangerous, costly and hypocritical energy policy. If the White House got its way, the energy conservation budget would have been slashed by 97 percent and the solar budget by 87 percent. The Solar and Conservation Bank would have been destroyed. State energy assistance and weatherization programs for low-income people would have been eliminated; appliance labeling, energy information programs and energy audits forgotten; and business energy tax credits repealed.

But while President Reagan used free enterprise rhetoric to justify solar and conservation reductions, he increased the nuclear budget, maintained synthetic fuel subsidies and granted of new tax benefits to the oil companies. If the White House gets its way, we will spend more on the military marching bands than on all solar and conservation efforts combined.

The Reagan plan is also bad for businesses. Both Japan and France now spend more per capita than the United States on solar energy development. And recent studies suggest tht foreign firms will soon capture the lucrative photovoltaics market, largely because the administration has abandoned the solar cell program.

But some of the most serious impacts of the Reagan energy plan affect individuals and families. By destroying the weatherization programs and the Solar and Conservation Bank, the administration would have hurt low-income people and hindering their hopes of cutting their energy costs. Without financial assistance, the poor cannot afford the up-front costs of conservation and solar improvements, despite the long-term economic benefits. It is a national disgrace that an estimated 1.5 million American homes went without heat or lights in 1982.

Although energy problems are national in scope, they vary within each state. But many states and communities are exporting, in energy costs, large amounts of capital. Those funds are not recycled within the local economy.

Until recently, few states had comprehensive energy plans. Confused by the national and international forces that determine energy supply and prices, most state legislatures set up only patchwork measures that use their energy more efficiently and develop some local renewable resources.

You can't directly attack motherhood, apple pie or solar energy. But renewable energy opponents contend that solar technologies are "exotic" fantasies that cannot produce useful energy until the 21st century. These critics ignore the fact that renewable energy sources (primarily hydroelectric dams and the burning of wood) supply more total energy than do all the nation's nuclear reactors. Even the Harvard Business School projects that solar technologies can soon supply more power than natural gas or coal and nuclear power combined.

Critics of energy conservation also argue that the nation needs more energy to fuel economic growth. But conservation means meeting our needs for lighting, warmth, mobility and industrial process energy in the most economic and efficient manner possible. Recent economic studies confirm that between 1973 and 1980, U.S. energy consumption rose by a total of only 2 percent. Over this same period, real Gross National Product -- corrected for inflation --- rose by 18 percent. Thus, almost 90 percent of the economic growth during these eight years was supported through increases in national energy productivity and only 10 percent through the introduction of additional energy sources.

Solar and conservation critics also maintain that government should not promote alternative energy development because the free market should be unfettered . Unfortunately, the energy market is anything but free. According to Battelle Institute, the federal government has given in the past more than $225 billion in subsidies to the coal, oil and nuclear power industries. Fourteen billion dollars in tax benefits are annually given to these industries. For solar and conservation measures to receive a fair shake, either all energy subsidies must be eliminated or a balanced energy program must be developed.

WHAT STATES CAN DO

The two major barriers to solar and conservation development are the lack of consumer education and the lack of financing.

Financing

° States should enact residential and business tax credits to stimulate energy conservation and for investment in solar and other renewable energy systems.

° States should develop programs that provide low interest loans to homeowners, multi-family buildings and businesses for energy conservation or for renewable energy improvements, either from direct government funds or through utility or commercial bank loans.

° States with severance taxes should use a percentage of their funds to finance energy development projects aimed at reducing the state's reliance on non-renewable energy.

° States should impose a surcharge on utility sales to finance independent corporations to fund renewable energy and conservation projects.

° States should increase the maximum loan limit to veterans for mortgages or homes equipped with renewable energy devices.

° States should stimulate alcohol fuels development by establishing tax credits for state residents who modify vehicles to use pure alcohol, waive the state sales tax on gasoline, provide grants and low-interest loans for small-scale alcohol production, and fund an extensive research program to identify new alcohol feedstocks.

Public Education

° States should provide information and/or training on solar and energy conservation for homeowners, landlords and businesses.

° States should initiate small grants programs for families and entrepreneurs who want to install conservation and renewable energy devices to offset high energy costs.

FOR FURTHER INFORMATION

Publications

New Initiatives in Energy Legislation: A State-by-State Guide, 1981-1982, 1982. Available for $5.95 from the Conference on Alternative State and Local Policies.

A New Prosperity: Building A Sustainable Energy Future, The Solar Energy Research Institute Solar/Conservation Study, 1982. Available for $20.95 from Brick House Publishing, 34 Essex St., Andover, MA 01810. The most comprehensive review of the potential for solar and conservation measures.

Power and Light: Political Strategies for the Solar Transition, David Talbot and Richard E. Morgan, Environmental Action Foundation, 1981. Available for $6.95 from the Pilgrim Press, 132 W. 31st St., New York, NY 10001.

Shining Examples: Model Projects Using Renewable Resources, Center for Renewable Resources, 1980. Available for $6.95 from the Center for Renewable Resources, Publications Department, 641 S. Pickett St., Alexandria, VA, 22304. Features 150 practical and creative community-based programs using conservation and renewable energy measures.

State and Local Solar Energy Policy: Meeting Low Income Needs, 1981. Available for $4.95 from the Conference on Alternative State and Local Policies.

Organizations

CONFERENCE ON ALTERNATIVE STATE AND LOCAL POLICIES, 2000 Florida Avenue, N.W., Washington, D.C. 20036 (202) 387-6030. Lee Webb, Director. Has an exclusive catalogue of publications including ones on solar and energy conservation.

ENERGY CONSERVATION COALITION, 1725 Eye Street, N.W., Suite 601, Washington, D.C. 20006 (202) 466-5045. Farwell Smith or David Moulton.

INSTITUTE FOR LOCAL SELF-RELIANCE, 1717 18th Street, N.W., Washington, D.C. 20009 (202) 232-4108. David Morris, Director.

NATIONAL CENTER FOR APPROPRIATE TECHNOLOGY, Box 3838, Butte, MT 59701 (406) 494-4572. Joe Sedlack, Director.

SOLAR LOBBY and the CENTER FOR RENEWABLE RESOURCES, 1001 Connecticut Avenue, N.W., Washington, D.C. 20036 (202) 466-6350. Scott Sklar, Director.

Prepared by Richard Munson.

Toxics

Toxic substances are everywhere in our environment. "The entire population of the nation and indeed the world, carries some body burden of one or several" toxins, according to a Library of Congress survey of chemical contamination.

More than 60,000 chemicals are in general commercial use and more than 1,000 new chemicals are developed annually. Yet only a few hundred of these chemicals are tested each year to determine whether they may be carcinogenic (cancer causing), mutagenic (causing genetic damage to the cells), teratogenic (causing damage to the developing fetus) or may result in other long-term adverse health effects.

No one escapes exposure to potentially hazardous chemicals.

Millions of workers are exposed to toxic substances in the workplace. Occupational exposure to these substances account for between 300,000 and 600,000 illnesses and deaths each year or about half of all occupational illnesses and deaths.

Consumers are exposed through produce laden with pesticide residues, through insulation emitting carcinogenic formaldehyde fumes and through hundreds of other products containing such substances as asbestos, benzidine-based dyes and chlorinated hydrocarbon solvents.

The four billion tons of chemicals transported each year by road, rail and waterway pose risks to communities of every size.

Everyone is at risk from improper disposal of the estimated 66 to 68 million pounds of hazardous waste generated each year. Of the 32,000 to 50,000 sites where such waste has been disposed, at least 2,000 pose significant environmental/health dangers and warrant quick remedial action. Hazardous waste particularly threatens ground water. About 50 percent of all Americans rely on ground water for their drinking water. Millions of citizens nationwide have had their municipal and private wells closed due to chemical contamination.

THE PROBLEM

Historians will probably mark 1983 as the year that environmental issues became central to American politics. Scandal at the EPA accomplished what many observers thought would be impossible: an avowedly probusiness, anti-regulatory administration was forced to commit itself to stricter federal controls on hazardous wastes. Yet toxics and the threat from toxics extends beyond the mammoth hazardous waste problem. Toxics problems begin with the manufacture of hazardous substances and continues through distribution, use and eventual disposal of those substances. Toxics are a widely-based, long-term problem. Toxics control requires a broad, integrated and long-range approach, which Washington cannot be solely relied upon to provide.

Unlike the infectious agents -- diptheria, smallpox, typhoid, polio -- that medical science has conquered in the last century, toxic chemicals generally produce effects that are difficult to recognize. Although some victims, such as small children, may experience immediate health problems, others exposed to toxic substances may not suffer health effects until many years after initial exposure. As many as 30 years may pass before the onset of cancer, leukemia or other health problems caused by toxic exposure. In some instances, health effects may even skip a generation.

These natural phenomenon are compounded by the fact that most medical doctors are not equipped to diagnose and treat diseases caused by exposure to toxic chemicals. A recent curriculum survey found that the average medical student receives less than four hours of training in industrial health during the entire four years of medical school. Independent occupational and environmental medicine specialists are increasing in number and their expertise is essential in enacting strong state and local laws to control toxic substances.

At least ten major federal laws cover various aspects of toxics control. Perhaps most important of these laws are the Toxic Substances Control Act (TSCA), the Occupational Safety and Health Act (OSHA), the Federal Insecticide, Fungicide and Rodenticide Act (FIFRA) and the Resource Conservation and Recovery Act (RCRA). TSCA covers the testing of new chemicals and existing chemicals; OSHA covers workplace hazards; FIFRA covers the sale and use of pesticides and RCRA calls for "cradle to grave" regulation of all wastes, including hazardous waste. In addition, the Comprehensive Environmental Response, Compensation and Liability Act (CERCLA) -- for which states must provide matching funds -- better known as Superfund, provides for the clean up of a limited number (400 sites) of abandoned hazardous waste dumps.

This formidable array of federal laws, however, has been undercut by massive budget and manpower cuts. The Occupational Safety and Health Administration seems to have abandoned its mandated objective of protecting worker health and safety, while its research and training arm, the National Institute for Occupational Safety and Health (NIOSH), is reeling under a 30 percent cut in funding. Most notably, the Environmental Protection Agency (EPA), with primary responsibility for TSCA, FIFRA, RCRA and Superfund has lost many of its best career scientists and enforcement personnel.

State officials have noted the impact of an eviscerated EPA. In a 1981 letter to a prominent environmental spokesman in Congress, James K. Hambright, president of the State and Territorial Air Pollution Program Administrators, wrote that "State programs need the technical support that EPA has provided in standard setting and strategy development. We must also have the backup of federal enforcement to ensure compliance with our regulations. Without strong EPA programs ...state programs will be largely ineffective."

As the "new EPA" struggles back onto its feet, the agency is receiving encouragement from environmentalists and industry alike. Even the industry journal, Chemical Week, admits that the federal government deserves to take a leading role in environmental protection: "Chemical industry operations must be safe and they must be widely perceived as safe. At this point the best route to both reality and perception is not a lot of PR smoke but credible watchdog agencies. One of those must be EPA, whatever it costs in the near term."

Aggressive and effective state actions to control toxics need strong federal toxic control programs. Federal programs, in addition to technical and enforcement support, provide overall standards for state, county and municipal efforts. Without federal standards, state and local toxic control can fall victim to destructive and "beggar thy neighbor" competition between the states or localities. As the vice president of one major hazardous waste management firm noted: "Unfortunately, it is clear that not all states will enact comprehensive preventive legislation if left to their own devices -- particularly if influenced by continued relaxation of federal guidelines. This relaxation means that increased quantities of hazardous waste will be landfilled in those states which have the weakest regulations and are, therefore, the least equipped to handle the hazardous waste problems which will arise in later years."

WHAT STATES CAN DO

Manufacturing Hazards

° States should pass legislation that would force industry to
reduce the amount of hazardous waste generated during production through such means as materials recovery, recycling,
and manufacturing process changes. Indiana, Kansas,
Kentucky, Maine, Missouri and Tennessee levy fees against
the generators of hazardous waste. Illinois offers tax-
exempt, low interest bonds for construction of facilities
engaged in "reducing, controlling or preventing pollution
...(or attempting to) reduce the volume or composition of
hazardous waste."

Protecting Workers and the Community

° States should pass right-to-know legislation that gives
workers and community residents the right to know the
identity and potential dangers of hazardous chemicals
used, stored or produced at local industrial firms. Right-
to-know laws in California, Connecticut, Maine, Maine, New
Hampshire, New York, Rhode Island and Wisconsin grant this
right, though only to workers.

Protecting Against Toxic Products

° States should pass legislation that will keep potentially
hazardous products from entering the marketplace. New
York and Massachusetts are considering legislation that
would require comprehensive labelling of consumer products,
in particular, school art supplies which have been found to
contain lead, asbestos, silica and other harmful substances
-- in the absence of adequate instructions for safe use.

Hazardous Waste Disposal

° States should pass legislation requiring that the safest
and most effective technologies are being used to manage
those wastes which cannot be reduced or recycled. California
has established a program that not only bans land disposal
of certain highly toxic wastes but also provides industry
with technical assistance to find alternative disposal and
reduction techniques.

Hazardous Waste Clean Up

° States should establish superfunds to clean up hazardous
waste dumps. Several states, including New Jersey, New
York, Minnesota, Missouri and California have passed state
superfund legislation. Money for these funds comes in
part from a tax levied against either generators or disposers
of hazardous waste.

FOR FURTHER INFORMATION

Publications

Exposure, national monthly news journal on waste and toxic issues. Available from Waste and Toxic Substances Project of the Environmental Action Foundation: $25 regular, $15 citizen group, $10 low-income or senior citizen, $50 business per annual subscription.

Fear at Work: Job Blackmail, Labor and the Environment, Richard Kazis and Richard L. Grossman, Pilgrim Press, New York, 1982.

Technologies and Management Strategies for Hazardous Waste Control, Office of Technology Assessment, March 1983. Landmark policy document. Available from U.S. Government Printing Office, Washington, D.C. 20402 (GPO stock no. 052-003-00899-8).

Waste and Toxic Substances Resource Guide, $2.00, Waste and Toxic Substances Project of the Environmental Action Foundation.

Winning the Right to Know: A Handbook for Toxics Activists, Caron Chess, 1983. Available from the Conference on Alternative State and Local Policies, 2000 Florida Avenue, N.W., Washington, D.C. 20009 (202) 387-6030. $7.95.

Organizations

CENTER FOR OCCUPATIONAL HAZARDS, 5 Beekman Street, New York, NY 10038 (212) 227-6220. Clearinghouse on occupational hazards, particularly those affecting artists and craftspeople.

ENVIRONMENTAL ACTION FOUNDATION, Waste and Toxic Substances Project, 724 Dupont Circle Building, Washington, D.C. 20036 (202) 296-7570. Operates national information clearinghouse on waste and toxic issues and publishes the monthly newsletter Exposure.

ENVIRONMENTAL DEFENSE FUND, 1525 18th Street, N.W., Washington, D.C. 20036 (202) 833-1484. Litigates on waste and toxics issues and does technical research.

NATIONAL COALITION AGAINST THE MISUSE OF PESTICIDES, 530 7th Street, S.E., Washington, D.C. 20003 (202) 543-4313, Jay Feldman.

OSHA/ENVIRONMENTAL NETWORK, Industrial Union Department, AFL-CIO, 815 16th Street N.W., Washington, D.C. 20006 (202) 842-7830. National political action and lobbying network of labor and environmentalists. Chapters in many states.

Prepared by James Lewis and Ken Silver.

Water and Sewers

America faces a national water crisis. It already exists in several areas of the country and it is likely to have an impact equal to or greater than that of last decade's energy crisis.

California, Connecticut, New Jersey and many other states have been hit with severe water shortages, which in many areas are exacerbated by toxic contamination. Underground water supplies across the country are being drained.

Many states face very serious water and sewage management problems in terms of higher costs for water and sewage services, reduced opportunities for economic growth and threats to public health.

Water and sewer systems are reaching the end of their design life in many of the nation's older cities. Cities and states will have to make repairs and replacements costing tens of billions of dollars. Repairing the hemorrhaging of New York City's 6,000 miles of sewers will cost billions. The federal government, whose policies more often promote the construction of new projects rather than the repair of existing systems, is unlikely to offer much assistance.

Many states' sewage policies discourage the use of treatment technologies that recycle water and wastes and use less energy -- systems that are especially appropriate and affordable. Traditional techniques have other high costs, including the unwanted, harmful development and needless loss of agricultural land and water.

Dangerous chemicals have contaminated drinking water and the food chain. Many states warn residents against eating fish from waters contaminated by chemical effluvia, including those of the Great Lakes and the Hudson and James Rivers. Water supplies in 29 percent of U.S. towns are contaminated with industrial chemicals, according to a recent EPA report.

The runoff of herbicides and pesticides from agricultural land and of metals and toxic organic materials from cities damages water quality throughout the country. States are on their own in finding solutions to these problems.

Workers at sewage treatment plants, hazardous waste and other environmental facilities often lack the training to manage sophisticated processes. Billions have been wasted constructing facilities which do not produce clean water or effective waste management because of improper operation and maintenance.

THE PROBLEM

While water problems vary from place to place, most fit
into one or more of the following patterns:

Money: Massive sums of money are needed for municipal
water and sewage treatment, infrastructure repair and replacement, the cleanup of toxic wastes and enforcement activities.
The bill for tackling these problems will fall, in large
part, onto state governments. Funding for the federal municipal
wastewater treatment construction grants program, for example,
has been cut by more than a third.

Funding for federal enforcement of major water protection
laws has also been sharply cut, leaving this difficult task to
the states. The Reagan administration's "New Federalism" program means that water quality programs are forced to compete
with desperately needed social programs. The country's
economic woes compound the problem, especially in many parts
of the Midwest and Northeast where the flight of capital is
most severe.

States can begin to seek alternate sources of money to
replace the traditional routes. Pension funds, cooperative
funding, lease-back arrangements, mixed private-public ventures,
revolving loan funds and a variety of ways to make scarce
public monies leverage larger sums of private capital are among
the policies that merit exploration.

Some control technologies are themselves revenue producing.
Hagerstown, Maryland is using its wastewater to grow trees
which will yield alcohol fuel.

Beyond deciding what kinds of projects to fund, states
and communities face hard decisions over where to target
their public dollars and the private dollars that follow.
Too often in the past much of the money has assisted new
suburban areas -- a policy promoted by powerful construction,
land, banking and development interests -- leaving less for
older central city areas most in need of pollution clean-up
and financial help. More conscious criteria are needed for
capital allocation to achieve the most cost-effective results
and to guard against this "sewer redlining." Needed too are
better mechanisms to permit concerned citizen groups to have
their voices heard and needs met in debates over where the
money goes.

High Tech vs. Appropriate Technology: Traditional responses to water problems have often meant expensive engineering solutions that failed to adequately recognize
resource limits. Building new sewage treatment plants, dams
to create a new water supply, and water diversion projects
often cost more and accomplish less than plugging leaky

sewers, preventing pollution, protecting groundwater recharge areas and conserving water in a myriad of other ways.

State policies are needed which aggressively encourage conservation, including permitting or even requiring water utilities to "front" the cost of water conservation devices for their customers and get the payback as part of the water bill process. Public grants and credit guarantees for a variety of activities, including new housing and building construction, can be conditioned on the maximum use of conservation techniques. In addition to saving dollars and water, appropriate technologies also create jobs.

Regulations: The problem of hazardous waste cleanup is economic, not technological. Companies like to skimp on clean-up costs, arguing that the economy is better served when their costs are less and their profits larger. This approach ignores costs to the communities in property and health damage. Moreover, it ignores the direct economic benefits -- including cleanup jobs, the commitment to continued operation that accompanies a polluter's investment in control technology and the recapture of valuable waste products currently thrown away -- that come with pollution controls.

Stronger law enforcement is one state weapon in the battle against toxic violence. Strict inspection and enforcement of dumping laws (financed by surcharges on industries generating potentially hazardous wastes) and broad right-to-know laws (informing workers and community residents of the chemicals they are exposed to) encourage more careful management.

Pricing: Distorted pricing policies which reward waste are at the root of many pollution and shortage problems. Changing to water "lifeline" rates (or other rate structures which charge large users more) helps protect poor and middle-income people, promotes conservation and raises more revenue from big users to finance safety improvements. It is especially important that large commercial users pay their fair share for water and sewer services. Pollution taxes -- fees based on the amount of waste discharged -- are no substitute for standards or prohibitions where dangerous toxics are concerned. But if combined with regulations, they could give a strong economic incentive for pollution control and may generate substantial revenue for the state as well.

WHAT STATES CAN DO

Encouraging Better Use of Water

° States should enact legislation to encourage more efficient uses of water. Legislation should encourage water-saving irrigation techniques, changes in plumbing codes to permit the use of water conservation devices and the establishment of rate structures that promote conservation, such as "lifeline" rates. California and New Jersey have created aggressive water conservation programs.

° States should encourage the use of sewage treatment techniques that use less energy and recycle water and wastes. In many states, changes in sanitary codes are necessary to allow these less costly techniques. New York, California and other states have passed legislation allowing creation of on-site wastewater districts. These districts provide rural areas with more flexible institutions to construct and manage on-site sewage treatment systems, like septic tanks. Michigan has passed a law to encourage the recycling of graywater (wastewater from showers and sinks).

° States should adopt policies to encourage recycling and reuse of wastewater and by-products of the treatment process. Preventing contamination by toxic substances is essential to promoting safe recycling of domestic wastewater. Colorado and other states have given priority to sewage treatment projects that recycle wastes.

Protecting Water Supplies

° States should map aquifer recharge areas and enact legislation to prevent development where the quality or quantity of underground water resources might be adversely affected. New York and Connecticut are examples of states that have begun to map their aquifers.

° States should limit the levels of, or ban phosphates altogether. Phosphate bans can be an effective means of reducing pollution and saving taxpayers money by lowering wastewater treatment costs. Michigan, New York and other states have limited phosphate levels in detergents.

° States should encourage stricter enforcement of water protection laws. Charging polluters and giving citizens an incentive to help enforce the law would stretch resources.

FOR FURTHER INFORMATION

Publications

    America In Ruins: Beyond the Public Works Pork Barrel, by
Pat Choate and Susan Walter, 1981, Council of State Planning
Agencies. A comprehensive survey warns that deteriorating
public facilities threaten national economic ruin unless new
ways are found to finance public works. Available from
Duke University Press.

    Building a Water Quality Consensus: Key Issues for the 80s.
Available from Margaret Downs at the Northeast-Midwest Institute,
218 D Street S.E., Washington, D.C. 20003 (202) 544-5200.

    Friday Morning Letter. The monthly newsletter of the
American Clean Water Association describes problems, solutions
and trends in the field of water and waste management.

    Participation in the Construction Grants Program: Accoun-
ting, Auditing and Financial Considerations. A practical
set of handbooks about sewage treatment. Available from
Arthur Young & Company, 227 Park Avenue, New York, NY, 10177
(212) 922-2100.

Organizations

AMERICAN CLEAN WATER ASSOCIATION, Larry Silverman, Executive
Director, 2025 I Street, N.W., Suite 519, Washington, D.C.
20006 (202) 293-0044. A professional association providing
technical assistance to communities on wastewater problems.

CLEAN WATER ACTION PROJECT, David Zwick, Executive Director,
733 15th Street, N.W., Suite 1110, Washington, D.C. 20005
(202) 638-1196. Public interest consumer lobby working on a
wide range of clean water and drinking water issues. CLEAN
WATER FUND, same address, (202) 638-3013, works with state
and local officials to help communities develop creative and
workable ways to finance their water and infrastructure needs.

ENVIRONMENTAL POLICY INSTITUTE, 317 Pennsylvania Avenue, S.E.,
Washington, D.C. 20003 (202) 547-5330. Research on water
conservation and analyses of state water conservation laws.
Contact Brent Blackwelder.

NATIONAL DEMONSTRATION WATER PROJECT, Edwin Cobb, Director,
1725 De Sales Street, N.W., Washington, D.C. 20036 (202) 659-
0661. NDWP and its affiliates around the country give practical
assistance to communities in solving water and waste problems
and train sewage workers.

Prepared by David Zwick and Ed Hopkins.

Human Services

Child Care

BACKGROUND FACTS

    The demand for high quality, reasonably-priced child care is growing. The government has significantly reduced its support for the care of children. By 1990, nearly 12 million pre-schoolers will need such care.

    Professional child care comes in two major forms: child care centers and child care homes. Home-based care is often called "babysitting" or more accurately, "family day care."

    While their parents work, at least 4.5 million children in this country spend the day in some form of unregulated child care.

    Of the estimated 6.2 million children in child care, only 900,000 are cared for in licensed day care centers. Some 5.3 million are kept in family day care homes, only 142,000 of which are licensed.

    Despite requirements in 40 states that family day care providers be licensed, certified or registered by a state agency, less than 10 percent of the estimated two million family day care homes in this country are so regulated.

    More than 4.5 million children receive child care in unregulated family day care homes from providers who may not be aware of basic health and safety requirements, nutrition information or the availability of resources for children.

    In addition, some parents of these four and a half million children may be ineligible for child care tax credits under the "Economic Recovery Act of 1981" because it requires that child care be provided in a licensed facility if the facility serves six children or more but says nothing about homes serving fewer than six children.

    State licensing standards have often reflected noble but unrealistic goals. Rather than encourage family day care providers to come forward in order to gain access to information, training and technical assistance (usually available at no cost to the taxpayer), strict and forbidding licensing and zoning requirements push providers further underground.

THE PROBLEM

There are two basic methods used by states to regulate family day care: licensing and registration.

Licensing is the granting of formal permission by a designated state or local agency to operate a child care facility. This agency has the authority to set standards, conduct inspections to ensure that standards are being met, establish procedures for revoking licenses and provide appeal mechanisms.

In addition to the inspections carried out by the licensing agency, local fire and health departments also conduct on-site inspections. Given limited state and local personnel, the licensing procedure is lengthy and sometimes expensive. Not only must state and local tax dollars be spent, but the provider herself often has to pay for the fire and/or health department inspections.

The common assumption is that licensed homes have been and continue to be monitored for various health and safety requirements such as fire inspections, cleanliness, emergency provisions, number of exits in the home, double sinks in the kitchen, number of children permitted in the home, fenced yards, separate cooking areas and planned child development activities. In reality:

° In 29 states, delays in on-site monitoring can mean that a family day care provider must wait for as long as one year to obtain her license or that her license will expire before it is renewed; and

° In 19 states, licensing requirements are so rigid and unrealistic that they act as a barrier to all but a few caregivers.

As a result, many more than four million children receive child care in unregulated family day care homes.

Registration is the other form of regulation that stresses caregiver self-inspection and parent awareness. When done properly, the process works as follows: registration standards, generally similar to those used in licensing, are determined by the state. When the family day care provider receives information detailing the standards, she/he does a self-study to determine whether or not the standards (including fire and health standards) are met and informs the state agency of her/his findings. Parents receive a copy of the regulations and a form for filing complaints. In many instances, inspections are not made unless the state receives a complaint.

Both licensing and registration offer some measure of the quality of child care provided and the physical condition of the homes. But such regulation of family day care has not been successful, as demonstrated by the fact that fewer than 10 percent of family day care homes are listed with a state agency, despite the existence of laws requiring such regulation in 40 states.

The quality of care <u>can</u> be improved however, through a registration process aimed at raising the level of awareness of both family day care providers and parents. In addition, once a provider is listed with a state agency:

° She/he gains access to information, training and technical assistance (generally offered by nonprofit organizations, organized family day care provider associations and universities to providers who can be reached by mail).

° As the provider becomes better informed about proper nutrition, the availability of toy lending libraries and assistance from provider associations, the quality of the care improves.

° Parents can check state lists and act as their own monitors and inspectors thereby helping other parents and children as well.

° Parents of children in these providers' care can be sure of their eligibility for the newly increased child care tax credit under the "Economic Recovery Tax Act of 1981."

Whatever the preference -- family day care homes or child care centers -- it is essential to protect the health and well being of children in care as well as to protect the rights of the child caregiver. In an economy that increasingly requires parents to work, it is incumbent upon state and local officials to propose and support measures that make as many forms of quality child care available as possible.

WHAT STATES CAN DO

Children and Youth Agency

° States should establish an agency for children and youth.
  In some states, like Massachusetts, this kind of agency
  is already established in the Governor's office. The
  agency should also provide services that support family
  day care homes such as: training and technical assistance
  to providers; referral services for providers and parents;
  a list of family day care providers to corporations and
  businesses for use by their employees; encouragement of
  day care centers to support and assist family day care
  homes; and inclusion of providers in conferences and boards
  of this agency.

Licensing and Registration

° States should alter their licensing and registration processes to allow for a more flexible registration process
  to encourage unregulated family day care providers to
  become regulated. All family day care homes should be
  required to register. Family day care homes should be
  monitored on a random sample and on the basis of complaints
  received. Georgia recognized this problem and after several
  years with a virtually unenforceable licensing law, switched
  to registration in 1980.

  In Texas, when licensing was in effect, only 15 to 20
  homes a month were licensed. Now with registration an
  average of 200 homes are registering with the state each
  month. Since registration was instituted in Massachusetts
  in 1974, the number of regulated homes has increased from
  862 to 5,100.

° States should encourage corporations and local businesses
  as well as nonprofit organizations, universities, etc.,
  to work with family day care providers and/or associations
  in developing their child care programs.

° States should establish outreach services aimed at encouraging
  providers to register. This should be done in cooperation
  with community groups, non-profit organizations concerned
  with child care and associations of family day care providers.

Zoning

° States should pass legislation creating a zoning variance
  that permits family day care homes to operate regardless
  of existing zoning regulations. Minnesota is among a
  number of states that has passed such a law. Unless this
  is done many providers will continue to operate outside of
  the law.

FOR FURTHER INFORMATION

Publications

Family Day Care Bulletin, published quarterly by The Children's Foundation, $8.00. A continuing review of programs, policy developments, laws and regulations.

Family Day Care Licensing Study, The Children's Foundation, $3.00. State-by-state analysis of licensing and regulation of family day care in the continental U.S.

Handbook of Family Day Care Associations, January, 1981, The Children's Foundation, $1.00. Annotated directory of state and local family day care associations.

Organizations

CHILD CARE LAW CENTER, 625 Market Street, Suite 816, San Francisco, CA 94105 (415)495-5498. Kathleen Murray and Carol S. Stevenson, Attorneys. A legal resource for the child care community including school age child care.

CHILD CARE RESOURCE CENTER, 187 Hampshire St., Cambridge, MA, 02139 (617) 547-9861. Works to expand the availability of parent and worker controlled child care, providing referrals and other support services.

THE CHILDREN'S FOUNDATION, 1420 New York Avenue, N.W., Suite 800, Washington, D.C., 20005 (202) 347-3300. Barbara Bode, President. A national organization working to ensure economic opportunity and access to decision-making processes for American families, particularly low- and moderate-income women and their children.

NATIONAL ASSOCIATION FOR FAMILY DAY CARE, 41 Dunbar Street, Manchester, NH 02103 (503) 622-4408. A provider-run association promoting the quality of family day care so that the best possible services are offered to children, parents and providers.

Prepared by Barbara Bode and Lori Weinstein.

Child Support Enforcement

BACKGROUND FACTS

One out of every two children today will live in a single parent home at some point during childhood. In those situations, 95 percent will live their mothers. Of the the children now living only with their mothers, 80 percent were born within a legal marriage.

The economic burden of providing for these children falls primarily upon the mothers. Although at least 3 1/2 million such women are due court-ordered child support from absent fathers, few of them receive what is owed. Only 49 percent of mothers in 1978 received the full amount due according to U.S. Census Bureau figures. Senator Malcolm Wallop (R-WY) recently said it was 25 percent. A well-known professional says it is six percent.

The earning potential of the average mother is 59 cents of the man and about half the children living in female-headed households currently live in poverty. In a major study of 3,000 California divorces, Dr. Lenore Weitzman found that one year after divorce, the average man's standard of living rose by 42 percent while that of his former wife and their children fell by 73 percent.

The "runaway pappy," at whom earlier decades' child support legislation was aimed, is no longer the unmarried, unemployed father. He is now the former husband and father, often middle class, who has simply left his family obligations behind. His children and their mother, however, like those in previous periods, have to turn to welfare for help.

In 1975, the Office of Child Support Enforcement (OCSE) was created within the U.S. Department of Health and Human Services under the new Title IV-D of the Social Security Act. This federal legislation sought to shift the burden of supporting children from the taxpayer to the natural parents and created within each state a IV-D agency, funded since 1982 by 70 percent federal dollars.

Neither the national system nor any state's courts are adequate to the present needs of custodial parents and their children or to the taxpayer. All research done on child support during the past decade agrees on several points:

(1) most fathers can pay child support; (2) fathers can usually pay more than courts order; (3) fathers who do pay, often do so irregularly and incompletely, creating recurrent financial hardship in the children's household; (4) one-fourth to one-third of fathers never make the first court-ordered payment; (5) no state or county has been found in which more than half the fathers are in full compliance with support orders.

THE PROBLEM

The need for full child support is obvious. The vast majority of absent fathers can pay that needed child support.

Prior to the establishment of OCSE, enforcement, as it was, was handled through a code -- the Uniform Reciprocal Enforcement of Support Act (URESA, later revised as RURESA). Every state has some form of URESA legislation, which mandates interstate cooperation in enforcing child support.

The complexity of the enforcement system, the variations in state laws, the geographic mobility of obligated fathers, crowded court dockets, budget and staff limitations within enforcement agencies and the fact that the system generally looks to the victim -- the mother acting on her children's behalf -- to push for enforcement of court orders have all created a situation in which married women and their children face a risk of poverty perhaps unprecedented in this country. In many ways, the present enforcement system supports, at all levels, the absent father's attitude that it's easier just to let the matter go.

The key policy issues for state government on child support enforcement are as follows: who owes it; where the obligated parent is; how much is owed; how and when it will be collected and disbursed; and what remedies are available when it is not paid.

° Who owes support: Before paternity is acknowledged or legally established, a father cannot be compelled to pay support and the mother is solely responsible. In 25 percent to 65 percent of cases, depending upon the area, legal establishment of paternity is an issue. Although exquisitely accurate methods of genetic determination of parenthood are available (HLA -- human leukocyte antigen -- and the less expensive serum protein and enzyme analysis), state laws and practices differ in accessibility and admissibility of this evidence of paternity. Legislation has been enacted in 32 states, however, providing for the introduction of the results of genetic testing in paternity hearings.

° Locating the absent parent: Once a support obligation is established, the obligated parent's whereabouts -- and assets -- must be known if a court order is to be enforced. Though federal and state parent locator systems exist, there are many problems with the timeliness of these services, costs to the custodial parent, and in some areas, the state's access to location information. Massachusets and Minnesota have enacted fairly strong legislation allowing disclosure of information to parent locator services.

° How much support is owed: Several different formulae have been proposed to determine equitable amounts of child support, each with advantages and disadvantages. Wide judicial latitude exists in setting amounts, however, and research indicates that orders are typically unrealistically low. The average amount is $1,800 a year. Further, mothers report that they fear seeking enforcement of support orders lest a new judge decrease the amount previously established, as an incentive for the father to pay; this seems particularly problematic in interstate cases.

° How and when support is collected and disbursed: Self-starting collection systems are clearly most effective. Michigan, the state with the best record, has had such a system through its Friend of the Court for decades. Only 10 states, however, have mandatory wage assignment laws and all wait until a delinquency has occurred; delinquent amounts tend to remain forever unpaid. A New York study showed that the payment rate on orders with a mandatory wage assignment provision was twice that (80 percent) of other orders. Five states still have no income withholding or assignment laws whatever.

The Internal Revenue Service and a number of states are now taking advantage of the new (1981 tax year) access to federal income tax refunds. Currently 16 states also provide for interception of state income tax refunds to repay AFDC support. In 1982, California collected nearly $13 million that way.

Payment of child support to a central agency, which then sends designated payments to the custodial household, both encourages and monitors compliance, saving the state and the custodial parent significant amounts of time and expense otherwise dependent on court hearings when delinquency occurs. Few states provide such a system. Timeliness is important. A court hearing can take months and custodial mothers who can't pay their rent can be evicted in a matter of weeks.

° Remedies for dealing with nonpayment: Swift, clear sanctions -- particularly jailing -- against nonpaying parents are essential to successful enforcement programs. In addition to wide variations in the remedies available from state to state, studies indicate the judges tend to be extraordinarily lenient with nonpaying fathers, perhaps reflecting the attitude that child support is basically a domestic matter rather than an economic and political issue of extreme importance.

WHAT STATES CAN DO

Statement of Legislative Intent

° States should pass legislation specifically affirming the fact that <u>both</u> parents are obligated for their children's support.

Child Support Clearinghouse

° States should establish a central agency through which all child support payments are made and disbursed thereby providing a current and accurate monitoring system. "Friend of the Court-type" systems with <u>trained</u> personnel and administrative processes to relieve the courts of unnecessary burdens should also be established.

Mandatory Wage Assignment

° States should pass legislation that requires payroll deductions of <u>all</u> child support obligations, with a court order going directly to the obligated parent's employer. The employer should be prohibited from penalizing the employee and be allowed to deduct minor administrative costs from the employee's pay.

Interception of Tax Refunds

° States should establish administrative procedures to intercept state and federal income tax refunds to repay arrearages for both AFDC and non-AFDC mothers alike.

Reduction of Judicial Latitude

° States should pass legislation requiring judges to use clear, timely and reliable sanctions for nonpayment; to prohibit reduction of support amounts as incentives to payment and prohibit forgiving of arrearages; to require enforcement of arrearages accrued in other states; and to require handling of interstate cases in a timely manner.

Child Support Advisory Committee

° States should establish an advisory committee -- with representation from enforcement agencies, the court system, the legislature and the affected citizenry -- to analyze and outline the state's needs for new legislation in such areas as establishing paternity, requiring the absent parent to provide health insurance in available, developing uniform and equitable formulae for amount of support obligations, prohibiting remarriage unless support is proven current, requiring security or bond on support orders, establishing lein effect of judgements and other issues determined to be necessary to an effective child support enforcement program.

FOR FURTHER INFORMATION

Child Support: An Overview, a six page fact sheet
available from the Children's Foundation. Singles are free,
.50 for additional copies.

Child Support Enforcement Bulletin. A quarterly review
of progress, problems and policy developments published by
the Children's Foundation. $8.00 a year.

A Guide to State Child Support and Paternity Laws: In
the Best Interest of the Child, by Carolyn R. Kastner and
Lawrence R. Young, 1981, National Conference of State Legislatures, 1125 17th Street, Suite 1500, Denver, CO 80202. A
guide to exemplary child support enforcement laws.

A Legislator's Guide to Child Support Enforcement, by
Carolyn K. Royce, 1980, National Conference of State Legislatures, 1125 17th Street, Suite 1500, Denver, CO 80202.
$5.00. A policy-oriented guide for legislators.

A Status Report of the Child Support Enforcement Program,
1983, National Council of State Child Support Administrators,
201 East Ninth Avenue, Suite 202, Anchorage, AK 99501. A
review of support enforcement together with policy recommendations from state agency administrators.

Organizations

CHILD SUPPORT ENFORCEMENT PROJECT, National Conference of
State Legislatures, 1125 17th Street, Suite 1500, Denver,
CO 80202 (303) 292-6600. Joan Smith, Project Director.
Technical assistance, information clearinghouse and publications
for state legislators.

THE CHILDREN'S FOUNDATION, 1420 New York Avenue, N.W., Suite
800, Washington, D.C. 20005 (202) 347-3300. Barbara Bode,
President. A national organization working to ensure economic
opportunity and access to decision-making processes for
American families, particularly low- and moderate-income
women and their children.

NATIONAL INSTITUTE FOR CHILD SUPPORT ENFORCEMENT (NICSE),
6110 Executive Boulevard, Suite 250, Rockville, MD 20852
(301) 984-9160. Technical assistance for child support
agencies, training courses, information and resource referrals.

Prepared by Worth Kitson Cooley.

The Elderly

BACKGROUND FACTS

Nearly 26 million people in the United States are 65 or older -- more than 11 percent of our total population.   In the last decade, the number of older Americans increased almost four times as rapidly as the under-65 age group (23.5 percent vs. 6.3 percent).

Each day, there is a net increase of 1600 Americans 65 or older. This translates to about a 600,000 annual increase in the 65-plus population.

The number of older Americans is expected to increase markedly in the years ahead, particularly during the first third of the 21st century. Almost 32 million Americans will be 65 or older by the year 2000. And by the year 2030 -- less than 50 years away -- more than 55 million persons in the U.S. will be 65 or older, which would constitute 18 percent of our total population.

Twenty-five percent of the population 65 or older (poverty and near poverty figures do not add because of rounding) were either poor or marginally poor in 1982. 3.9 million were actually <u>below</u> the poverty line ($4,400/year).

Older Americans are subject to more disability, see physicians 50 percent more often and have twice as many hospital stays that last almost twice as long as those of younger persons.

In 1981, Medicare spending for the elderly totaled $44.8 billion. Per capita health spending was $3,140 for every person 65 or older, as compared to the $828 per capita average for an under-65 individual.

Many older Americans now find themselves in virtually impossible housing situations. Rising enery costs, property taxes and maintenance expenses are making it difficult for them to remain in their homes.

Older women constitute 59 percent of all Americans 65 or older, but equal nearly 72 percent of all the aged persons living in poverty. About 19 percent of all women 65 or older were poor in 1980, compared to 11 percent for older men. The overall poverty rate for persons 65 and older was 15.3 percent in 1981.

THE PROBLEM

To be an older person in America today is to be subject
to a growing array of frustrations and problems. Along with
the problems that every American faces, the elderly confront
the additional problem of maintaining their standard of
living, with limited resources, fixed incomes and fragile
health.

A few examples illustrate the range of difficulties
older people face each day:

° Condominium conversion of rental properties occupied by
  senior citizens requires them to find inexpensive, convenient,
  safe residences in a tight housing market.

° Cutbacks in transportation services and subsidies strand
  persons who cannot or will not drive. Transportation is
  an even more serious problem in rural areas with little
  public transportation.

° Rising costs in energy, food, housing and health care,
  coupled with reductions in programs designed specifically
  for the elderly in these areas, force them to make impossible
  choices among necessities.

° Age discrimination and high levels of unemployment limit
  income potential.

Of all the problems encountered by the elderly, obtaining
adequate and reasonably-priced health care is one of the most
pressing. Health care costs are growing at twice the rate
of the rest of the economy with the elderly accounting for
an increasing share of the bill.

The elderly's acute health care (short-term) needs are
largely satisfied by Medicare. However, because their
problems are often chronic, many older people also need long-
term care services not generally required by the younger
population. Consequently, the need for -- and current lack
of -- long-term care services is an especially critical
problem.

Long-term care includes a range of medical and supportive
services for individuals who have lost some capacity for self-
care due to a chronic illness or condition. At present,
long-term care is typically associated with nursing homes.
Nursing homes, however, are often not "homes" but sterile,
impersonal institutions providing substandard care. And
while only five percent of the elderly population reside in

nursing homes, up to 50 percent of these people could receive care more appropriate to their conditions outside a nursing home.

Despite the public perception of nursing homes as the major provider of long-term care, the vast preponderance of care for the elderly is provided by family and friends. To aid these caregivers and for the elderly person living alone, there should exist a wide range of community-based services designed specifically for the elderly. Such services should include adult day care, in-home care, homemaker/chore services, personal care, counseling and nutritional programs. To a very limited extent, these services are available through such programs as the Community Services Block Grant (formerly Title XX) and the Older Americans Act.

Unfortunately, because resources are so limited, in many states alternative services that would allow the elderly to remain at home do not exist or are rare. This often requires premature and inappropriate admission to a nursing home. Once in the nursing home, the older person may suffer not only from chronic illness, but also from questionable care and treatment.

In response, state governments have enacted a wide range of long-term care programs. To address the problems found in their nursing homes, Illinois, Minnesota and Michigan have enacted nursing home reform legislation that regulates and attempts to improve the quality of care. A number of other states, such as Connecticut, Washington and Florida have provided funding to establish community-based service systems for the elderly.

Critics claim that providing a coordinated system of care will increase public costs. Inevitably they say, many elderly persons who now need these services but do not have access to them would use them. However, the availability of these services could preclude the necessity of more costly nursing home admissions in a significant number of cases, thus saving money in the long run.

WHAT STATES CAN DO

Provide Long-Term Care in the Least Restrictive Setting:

° States should adopt a Medicaid provision that covers a
  wide range of home- and community-based services as an
  alternative to nursing home care. This would help reduce
  the institutional bias associated with Medicaid.

° States should provide funds to develop or maintain service
  programs to prevent premature, inappropriate institution-
  alization of the elderly. These could be home-delivered
  services, multi-service senior center programs, family
  placement service programs and/or day care programs.

° States should allow family allowances, personal care reimbursement, tax deductions and/or tax credits for families
  that provide major support to an elderly person. This
  would be incentive for families to continue to care for
  elderly relatives at home.

° States should create a State Joint Committee on Long-Term
  Care Alternatives to study their costs and effectiveness.

Protect Rights of Residents and Ensure Quality of Care in
Institutions:

° States should enact comprehensive laws regulating nursing
  homes. Provisions should, for example, include access to
  facilities by visitors, a residents' bill of rights, nursing
  aid training requirements and enforcement measures.

° States should establish a nursing home ombudsman program
  to oversee nursing home activities and investigate complaints.

Ensure Availability of Appropriately Trained Health Care
Providers:

° States should require physicians, osteopaths and chiro-
  practors to indicate whether they will accept Medicare
  reimbursement as payment for services to Medicare eligibles.

° States should enact upgraded geriatric licensing laws for
  physicians, nurses and other professionals who treat the
  elderly.

Protect the Elderly from Questionable Insurance Sales Tactics:

° States should enact laws strictly regulating the sale of
  health insurance policies sold to supplement Medicare.
  This would protect the elderly from the cost of duplicative
  policies and unnecessary coverage.

FOR FURTHER INFORMATION

Publications

Alternatives to Institutional Care for the Elderly: An Analysis of State Initiatives, Gail Toff. Published by the Intergovernmental Health Policy Project of George Washington University. Describes successful state programs.

Legislative Approaches to Problems of the Elderly: A Handbook of Model State Statutes, Legislative Research Center of the University of Michigan Law School, Ann Arbor, MI, William J. Pierce, Director. March 1971.

Living in a Nursing Home: A Complete Guide for Residents, Their Families and Friends, Sarah Greene Burger and Martha D'erasmo.

Long-Term Care, Background and Future Directions, U.S. Department of Health and Human Services, Health Care Financing Administration, 1981. General information about long-term care.

Organizations

AMERICAN ASSOCIATION OF RETIRED PERSONS, 1909 K Street, N.W., Washington, D.C. 20049 (202) 872-4200. Has a state legislation department active in elderly issues across the country.

BUREAU OF AGING, Department of Social and Health Services, OB-43G, Olympia, WA 98504 (206) 753-2502. Administers the Senior Citizens Services Act, enacted in 1976.

CENTER FOR COMMUNITY CHANGE, Coalition on Block Grants and Human Needs, 1000 Wisconsin Avenue, N.W., Washington, D.C. 20007 (202) 333-0822. Monitors state activity involving implementation of block grants.

NATIONAL CITIZENS COALITION FOR NURSING HOME REFORM, 1309 L Street, N.W., Washington, D.C. 20005 (202) 393-7979. Expertise on nursing home issues, including state legislative activities.

NATIONAL COUNCIL OF SENIOR CITIZENS, 925 15th Street, N.W., Washington, D.C. 20005 (202) 347-8800. Advocates on behalf of the elderly, with expertise in health and housing issues.

OFFICE OF AGING AND ADULT SERVICES, Department of Health and Rehabilitataive Services, 1321 Winewood Blvd., Tallahassee, FL 32301 (904) 488-8341. Responsible for implementing recently enacted Community Care for the Elderly Act.

Prepared by Joanna Chusid.

Health Care

The United States spends enormous amounts on health. In 1980, health care expenditures in the United States totaled $247.2 billion -- an average of $1,067 per person. Health care expenditures were 9.5 percent of the total gross national product.

Health costs continue to rise. The consumer price index for medical care has been increasing at a rate of 10 to 12 percent per year.

Government health care programs are extensive. Medicaid pays for the medical care of 25 million elderly persons, 5 million disabled persons, 9 million poor children, and 4 million unmarried, low-income parents.

Most government health care expenditures are for institutional care. In 1980, for example, hospital care accounted for 74 percent of all Medicare expenditures.

Despite the high level of expenditures in the United States -- public and private -- on health care, major problems remain. And those problems are not shared equally. Major differences in health care between rich and poor, and between black and white are a serious national problem. For example:

° Child deaths, death from chronic diseases (stroke, peptic ulcers, bronchitis, respiratory cancers, and cancers of the stomach and esophagus) and deaths from accidents are all more common among the economically deprived.

° The infant mortality rate continued to decline, reaching 13.8 deaths per 1,000 live births in 1978. The mortality rate for black infants, however, is still almost twice as high as for white infants. And now areas with high unemployment are starting to see a reversal of the trend.

° Age-adjusted mortality rates continue to decline. However, in 1978, they remained 80 percent higher for men than for women and 48 percent higher for blacks than for whites.

° Use of doctors offices and hospital clinics is considerably lower in nonmetropolitan areas. Furthermore, residents of counties that did not have a city with a population of 10,000 or more generally had lower usage rates than other nonmetropolitan areas.

THE PROBLEM

One of the biggest problems of American health care is that it focuses on treatment and cure, rather than on prevention.

Hospital care expenditues continue to claim the largest share of the health care dollar, accounting for 40 percent of total health care expenditures in 1980. Physician services and nursing home care accounted for 19 percent and 8.4 percent respectively.

Less than two percent of health expenditures go toward public health programs such as childhood immunizations, venereal disease and tuberculosis control, fluoridation, family planning, community mental health centers and alcohol and drug abuse treatment. Yet these programs are far more cost-effective than hospital care.

Public health programs targeted at special health problems of special populations have contributed to the improved health of Americans and have reduced the discrepancies between rich and poor, white and non-white, and urban and rural Americans. These programs suffer as hospital care and nursing home care consume most of the health budgets.

One major consequence of the medical thinking has been the denigration of active prevention efforts. Instead of looking for health problems that can be prevented by social action (such as cleaning up water supplies and removing hazardous wastes), there is a new focus on individual life-styles. This "blame the victim" approach makes it the responsibility of the worker to protect himself from hazards in the workplace; the responsibility of the individual to quit smoking, to eat correctly, and to exercise; and, when disease strikes, the responsibility of the victim for having failed to prevent it. State leaders must reinstate the proper policy role for effective public health programs if we are to preserve the health of our people.

States have always been responsible for public health. The federal government has contributed funds, but state governments have had the basic statutory responsibility for health. The federal medical care programs -- Medicare and Medicaid -- have grown far more rapidly than public health.

Medical care costs: The growing public demand for medical services has been fostered and responded to by a growing medical establishment. Health is the second largest sector of the economy; in many towns or cities hospitals are the largest employers. This has made it almost as difficult to redirect the medical establishment as to trim the military-industrial complex.

The "national health tax" -- the combination of tax money spent on government health programs and health insurance premiums paid by corporations and individuals -- is the second largest "tax" system after the personal income tax. Yet, unlike actual tax money, these funds are spent without deliberation, without planning, and without accountability.

Because medical care is so expensive, the right to medical care is critical for almost everyone. Great progress has been made in assuring access to medical care. Massive income transfers take place through private health insurance and government health insurance (Medicare and Medicaid).

The problem best addressed at the state level is protecting the right to medical care -- but without unintended growth of non-productive parts of the health establishment. Hospital costs are still rising at the rate of 18 percent per year.

Enforcement of the public commitment to health: There is strong evidence from opinion polling that the American people are deeply committed to protecting the public health. They oppose weakening of environmental and public health statutes. Yet state leaders have been slow to recognize the opportunity to strengthen laws and programs. For example, at a recent meeting of state health officers, the prevailing fear about toxic wastes was labeled "public hysteria." Repeatedly these public health officials admitted to themselves the real danger, but were unwilling to undertake a program to manage the hazard because of the fear that they could not deal with the public response.

Nursing homes have been a national scandal for almost two decades, yet the Reagan administration has proposed deregulating the industry. It is an industry where the profit comes from the real estate transactions and where patients -- the most vulnerable people in our society -- are often abused or neglected. The public would like stronger protections. Because the abuses are still so clear, there is room for aggressive reform.

WHAT STATES CAN DO

Public Health

° States should give public health and prevention the highest
priority in their planning and budgeting. To do this, states
must analyze and duplicate the programs that work such as
immunizations, fluoridation, feeding programs (WIC), and
crippled childrens' programs; maintenance programs for the
elderly; and programs for protection from environmental
hazards.

Health Costs

° States should act to increase the accountability of Blue
Cross/Blue Shield (dominated by physicians and other
health industry professionals) to the public as a means of
controlling rapidly rising health insurance costs. Michigan
law requires that three-quarters of "the Blues'" state
board of directors be subscribers.

° States should institute "rate setting" programs to review
hospital budgets and control the rates of growth of expenditures. Such initiatives have been successful in Maryland,
Massachusetts and New Jersey. These programs are most
effective when linked to certificate of need programs that
allocate new capital expenditures for the provision of needed
services.

° States should encourage health maintenance organizations
(HMOs) which discourage the use of expensive hospital services, while providing more benefits in ambulatory care
than normal insurances.

Enforcement

° States should strengthen enforcement programs to protect
public health. Tough law enforcement programs to attack
problems such as toxic waste dumps, substandard nursing
homes, radiation hazards and air pollution could produce
improvements in public health.

Home Health

° States should adopt home health plans for the elderly and
mentally retarded under waivers from Medicaid institutional
care requirements. Kansas, Montana, Oregon and Louisiana
have received waivers to reimburse the cost of home health
care as an economical alternative to institutional care.

FOR FURTHER INFORMATION

Publications

"Who Needs Medicaid?" David E. Rogers, Robert J. Blendon and Thomas W. Moloney, New England Journal of Medicine, Vol. 307, July 1, 1982.

A New Perspective on the Health of Canadians, Marc Lalonde, National Health and Welfare, Ottawa, Canada, 1974. Good overview of preventable health problems.

A Pro-Competitive Model for a Statewide Health Insurance Program: The Oregon Proposal, Lynn S. Katzman and Robert O'Brien, 1983. A Policy Memo available for #3.50 from the Conference on Alternative State and Local Policies, 2000 Florida Avenue N.W., Washington, D.C. 20009.

Organizations

AMERICAN PUBLIC HEALTH ASSOCIATION, 1015 15th Street, N.W., Washington, D.C., 20005 (202) 789-5600. APHA also has about 50 state affiliates.

CENTER FOR POLICY RESEARCH, National Governor's Association, 444 N. Capitol Street, Washington, D.C., 20001 (202) 624-5354. The Center has a State Medicaid Information Center and sponsors research on state health policy.

CHILDREN'S DEFENSE FUND, 122 C Street N.W., Washington, D.C., 20001 (202) 628-8787.

INTERGOVERNMENTAL HEALTH POLICY PROJECT, George Washington University, Washington, D.C. 20006. Publishes State Health Notes monthly and other reports occasionally.

NATIONAL ASSOCIATION OF COMMUNITY HEALTH CENTERS, INC., 1625 Eye Street, N.W., Suite 420, Washington, D.C. 20006 (202) 833-4280. Clearinghouse for information on community health center legislation and budgets.

PUBLIC CITIZEN HEALTH RESEARCH GROUP, 2000 P Street, N.W., Seventh Floor, Washington, D.C., 20036, (202) 872-0320. Publishes numerous studies on health care policy, drugs and medical technology.

Prepared by Anthony Robbins.

Housing

<u>BACKGROUND FACTS</u>

The U.S. faces a major housing crisis. Annual housing starts continue at one of their lowest rates in history. The construction of rental housing falls further and further behind demand.

Consumers must pay increasing portions of their income for housing. Interest rates remain very high; and savings and loan associations -- the traditional source of financing for housing -- are in trouble.

Housing starts in the U.S. are down because interest rates are high. Housing starts in 1982 were about 950,000 units nationwide -- almost 35 percent less than the 1.3 million starts in 1980. The rental unit construction has dwindled since the early 1970s because costs of construction surpass renters' ability to pay. Federal cut-backs in subsidized rental housing programs further diminished the rental construction rate.

The effective mortgage interest rate for conventional new homes is now 13 percent. High interest rates are preventing developers from building marketable housing and stopping consumers from buying new or existing housing. High interest rates have caused a 25 percent decline in rehabilitation nationwide.

Demolitions and condominium conversions are shrinking the number of rental units while rental costs continue to climb. Rent to income ratios are steadily rising. In 1950, 32 percent of all renters paid more than 25 percent of their income for rent; in 1979, more than half did. Affordability is an especially serious problem for low- and moderate-income families.

Savings and loans are in trouble. Rising inflation has presented many lenders with serious cash flow problems. Interest rates due on deposits have risen to high levels, but interest received on mortgages and other assets lags.

The Reagan administration wants to cut back nearly every federal housing program. A third of his recommended 1982 budget cuts were targeted at federally-assisted housing programs. The administration also wants to slash financing for construction and rehabilitation of sewers, streets and water systems.

THE PROBLEM

The current nationwide housing crisis has been created by a complex set of problems, particularly:

Affordability: Home prices are so high that first-time homebuyers cannot accumulate a sufficient down payment nor can they make monthly payments at current interest rates. And renters have to pay increasing portions of their incomes for rent -- leaving less money for food and medical care.

Availability: Construction of all types of housing is down, particularly in fast growing areas such as the Sunbelt. Builders can't afford to build.

Financing: High interest rates stop new construction. Savings and loans find few borrowers for their loans. The long-term, fixed rate mortgages are few and far between.

Quality: Housing in many parts of the country is in poor condition and needs to be rehabilitated. Multi-family housing, particularly in the northeast, is in very bad condition.

Displacement: Demand for housing in areas close to central cities is skyrocketing. Many lower-income people are displaced from their inner-city neighborhoods through rent increases, evictions or through condominium conversions.

Speculation: Demand for housing as both an investment and as a tax shelter drives prices up. Speculation keeps boosting the price of land and buildings.

Tenants: More and more families expect to be tenants all their lives. They think of themselves as tenants, not future homeowners.

State officials must find solutions to housing problems and fight to keep the federal government involved in housing financing. They need continued access to mortgage revenue bonds.

State strategies on how to deal with the housing crisis may take a variety of forms such as: permitting innovative local land use and regulatory techniques at the local level; preventing exclusionary zoning; promoting expedited permit processes; making land and infrastructure available for housing; promoting the use of manufactured housing; promoting building codes that protect health and welfare but do not add excessive costs; financing construction and rehabilitation of housing; strengthening landlord-tenant law to increase tenant protection; and promoting cooperative ownership arrangements.

With federal cutbacks, the state programs may be the "only game in town." States should actively initiate financing programs that maximize the use of federal funds that are responsive to local needs.

In these times of fiscal austerity, regulatory approaches and programs to make maximum use of existing housing should also be tried. Saving a community's affordable housing is far cheaper than subsidizing new construction. Because funds for new construction are limited, states should not stand in the way of local ordinances that control rents, condominium conversions, speculation, and inclusionary zoning. Also, local ordinances that permit splitting up single family homes for "second units" should not be prevented by state action. State legislation permitting innovative local land use and regulatory techniques should be passed.

There are two traditional arguments against federal and state housing programs: 1) that they cost too much; and 2) the private market can take care of the problems of low- and moderate-income people.

Proponents of federal and state housing financing argue that the free market does not take care of all housing problems -- and therefore, government action is necessary. Nor are housing programs terribly expensive; the funds spent on low- and moderate-income housing programs are nowhere near the funds lost to the U.S. Treasury through mortgage interest deductions.

Opponents of the idea of local governments using their regulatory powers to conserve low-and moderate-income housing charge that these local initiatives thwart the "free market" and keep it from providing housing for all income groups. Proponents of these regulatory initiatives such as rent control, condominium conversion, demolition ordinances and inclusionary zoning reply that the private market often does not meet the needs of low- and moderate-income people. Thus such policies are needed to conserve affordable housing.

WHAT STATES CAN DO

Encouraging Affordable Housing at the Local Level

° States should pass legislation encouraging innovative local government ordinances such as mixed use development, density bonuses, inclusionary zoning and the division of single family homes for second units. California has passed legislation requiring localities to grant a 25 percent increase in permitted density in project where 25 percent of the units will be affordable for low- and moderate-income people.

° States should prevent zoning techniques that effectively exclude low or moderate income families or individuals.

° States should encourage local ordinances that conserve affordable housing, such as rent control and condominium conversion.

° States should promote expedited permit processes. Virginia mandates a maximum of 120 days for decisions on all subdivision permits. California permits local governments to consolidate all permits into one administrative process.

Financing Housing

° States should help finance housing. California operates numerous housing finance programs. Connecticut, Minnesota and Wisconsin operate active rehabilitation funds. New Jersey operates a neighborhood improvement program. Connecticut, North Carolina and California are exploring the use of public pension funds for purchase of mortgage backed, pass-through securities. California and Hawaii permit use of public pension funds for state employees' mortgages.

° States should make land and infrastucture available for housing. Connecticut, Florida and California all provide low-interest loans for the purchase and development of land for low- and moderate-income housing.

Protecting Tenants

° States should strengthen tenant protection. New Jersey has strong just-cause eviction protections. Twelve states require interest to be paid to tenants on security deposits.

° States should promote cooperative ownership. New York and California have encouraged the financing and development of cooperatives for low- and middle-income people.

FOR FURTHER INFORMATION

Publications

Housing Affairs Letter, newsletter published by Community Development Publications, 8555 16th St., Silver Spring, MD 20910.

The Housing Crisis: A Strategy for Public Pension Funds, Robert Schur and Marilyn Phelan, 1982. Available for $5.95 from the Conference on Alternative State and Local Policies.

Moderate Rent Control: The Experience of U.S. Cities, John Gilderbloom, 1980. Available for $4.95 from the Conference on Alternative State and Local Policies.

Packaging Mortgage Loans: Strategies for California, John C. Harrington, 1980. Available for $5.95 from the Conference on Alternative State and Local Policies.

Rent Control: A Source Book, John Gilderbloom and Friends, 1981. Available for $9.95 from the Conference on Alternative State and Local Policies.

Shelterforce, available to individuals at $8 for 6 issues, $12 to libraries, law offices and institutions, 380 Main St., East Orange, NJ 07018.

State Actions for Affordable Housing, prepared for HUD Office of the Assistant Secretary for Policy Development and Research, Washington, D.C.

Organizations

HOUSING ASSISTANCE COUNCIL, INC., 1025 Vermont Avenue, N.W., Suite 606, Washington, D.C. 20005 (202) 842-8600.

NATIONAL HOUSING LAW PROJECT, 2150 Shattuck Avenue, Suite 300, Berkeley, CA 94704 (405) 548-9400.

NATIONAL LOW-INCOME HOUSING COALITION, 215 Eighth Street, N.E., Washington, D.C. 20002 (202) 544-2544.

NATIONAL TENANTS UNION/SHELTERFORCE, 380 Main Street, East Orange, NJ 07018 (201) 678-6778. Membership organization of housing activists and public officials.

PLANNERS NETWORK (Housing and Neighborhoods Task Force), P.O. Box 4671, Sather Gate Station, Berkeley, CA 94704.

Prepared by Marilee Hanson and Leonard Goldberg.

Crime

Criminal Justice

BACKGROUND FACTS

    Violent crime in the United States is a continuing social disaster.

    Thirty-three out of every thousand Americans were the victims of some violent crime in 1980.

    By the beginning of the 1980s, an American's chances of being murdered were roughly eight to 12 times those of citizens of most other advanced European countries.

    Though the threat of criminal violence crosses all social, economic and geographic boundaries. But, it is much more severe for some groups and in some places than others. It is more an urban problem than a rural or suburban one. It is more threatening to the young than to the middle-aged and elderly. And it is more a fact of life for the poor and minority than for the affluent and white.

    And though no state has been spared the fear and anguish that serious crime brings, the scale of the problem is different across different states; different in New York, for example, where the homicide rate is about 12 per 100,000 per year, than in Minnesota, where the rate is about 2 per 100,000.

    Both the public and elected officials believe that crime has increased drastically in the last few years. Newsweek for instance, argued in 1981 that we are suffering an "epidemic" of violent crime. Problems of reporting and measuring crime make precise estimates of trends over time difficult. Interestingly though, the FBI's official statistics indicate that nationally, rates of serious violent crime probably leveled off during the mid-1970s and increased somewhat thereafter, reaching a recent peak in 1980 with slight, irregular declines since then. Surveys of the victims of crime undertaken by the National Institute of Justice suggest a more stable pattern for most crimes, at least through 1981.

    Violent crime takes an enormous toll -- not only in injuries and death, but also in pervasive and often crippling fear in many communities and in the massive diversion of scarce public resources into police, courts and prisons.

    State governments alone spent almost $4.5 billion on corrections in 1980 -- more than they spent on all natural resources programs, more than twice what they spent on employment security and more than 10 times what they spent on corrections in 1960.

THE PROBLEM

In the last several years, most legislative initiatives against crime have emphasized "getting tough" with criminals. States have adopted stiff, mandatory sentences for repeat offenders or those who use weapons; they have allowed for even very young criminals to be tried in adult criminal courts; and they have established harsh penalties for drug offenses.

The most dramatic expression of this mood has been the recent passage in California of a "Victim's Bill of Rights" (Proposition 8) that mandates a wide range of major changes in that state's criminal justice policy. Proposition 8's provisions ranged from the abolition of felony plea-bargaining, to heavy restrictions on the right to bail, to a vague provision enforcing the right of children to attend "safe" schools.

These "get tough" policy initiatives are based on two interrelated assumptions. The first and most common is that American criminal justice is "soft" on criminals; crimes are committed because the "costs" of committing a crime have gone down drastically. The second is that there is little government can do to reduce crime rates. Programs to rehabilitate offenders, in this view, are uniformly failures and the experience of the 1960s "proves" that such measures as employment and training programs and antipoverty efforts cannot prevent crime.

Though few people would disagree that we need an efficient and effective criminal justice system, the premise that our current system is "soft" -- and that we can stop crime by getting still "tougher" -- is wrong. The harsher policies of the past several years in fact, must be seen as an experiment that has largely failed.

By December, 1982, the state and federal prison population stood at an all-time high of 412,000 -- up an astonishing 110 percent since 1970 and up by 43,000 from the end of 1981 alone. In early 1983, 31 states were under court orders to reduce serious prison overcrowding; California was preparing to house some state inmates in tents. Yet this dramatic increase in prison population has had no discernible effect on rates of serious crime.

The United States has 180 per 100,000 of its citizens in prison, a far greater than any comparable industrial society. Yet our rates of serious violent crime remain far higher. The two industrial nations with higher proportions in prison are ones with huge populations of political prisoners -- the Soviet Union and South Africa. The Dutch rate of imprisonment, in the late 1970s, was 18 per 100,000.

Some of the states in America with the highest rates of
imprisonment -- with the highest "costs" of crime -- are also
those with some of the highest rates of serious violent crime.
Georgia imprisons people at a rate over five times that of New
Hampshire and has six times New Hampshire's homicide rate.
North Carolina has five times the imprisonment rate of Minnesota
and over four times the murder rate. New York's imprisonment rate
is more than double the rate in Massachusetts, and it has more than
triple the murder rate. Nevada has both the third highest imprisonment rate and the highest murder rate of any state in the union
excluding the District of Columbia.

In general -- though some particular jurisdictions may be
excessively lenient with offenders -- the failure of the
criminal justice system to deal sharply with "hard-core" or
"career" offenders is not the main problem. Sometimes,
these criminals do "fall through the cracks" of the justice
system -- but not often. Several studies have found for
example, that repeat violent offenders have about a nine in ten
chance of imprisonment once convicted in the jurisdictions
studied. A major evaluation of special "career criminal"
programs -- designed to give prosecutors more resources to
deal more effectively with repeat offenders -- found that
the programs had unexpectedly small effects, because the
prosecutors were already doing a good job of putting repeat
offenders away. (The often lax treatment of family violence
-- especially of men who assault their wives -- is a frequent
exception to this general point.)

The much more significant problem is that most crimes do
not even result in an arrest. One RAND Corporation study of
repeat felons in California found that their chances of being
arrested for any one robbery were about one in ten. To change
this pattern significantly, we would need to develop dramatically more effective police strategies; but despite considerable
research no one has yet come up with those strategies.

The relative failure of these strategies points to the
need to think much more realistically about the limits of
criminal justice systems -- by themselves -- in fighting
crime. (A credible anti-crime strategy must, therefore,
emphasize a broader range of interventions.)

Most progressive approaches share common themes. They
recognize the need to make criminal justice as fair and
effective as possible. They try to move outside the justice
system altogether and intervene directly in the neighborhood
and family situations that more clearly affect crime rates.
None of them are panaceas for urban crime; but all of them
show promise in reducing crime or, at the very least, in
reducing a community's fear and sense of powerlessness about
crime. They emphasize building local participation and
they are relatively inexpensive as compared to spending on
more traditional criminal justice.

WHAT STATES CAN DO

Community Prevention

° States should help evaluate and implement local community dispute
  resolution programs, typified by San Francisco's Community Boards
  program, which trains local people to mediate disputes among
  neighbors, family members and others, thus reducing pressure
  on the formal criminal justice system.

° States should develop programs to link employment, training and
  education programs for offenders and high-risk youth with broader
  strategies of locally-based economic development. The most promi-
  long-run strategy against crime involves local development programs
  that can help maintain crucial family and community networks while
  offering the realistic chance of stable, long-term employment.

° States should promote "neighborhood watch" programs to encourage community residents to become involved in anti-crime
  programs. Although studies of the effectiveness of such
  programs have come up with mixed results, some local programs
  are thought to have been successful in reducing some forms of
  crime and in boosting community involvement.

Family Interventions

° States should support the development of comprehensive
  family service programs, exemplified by the Child and Family
  Resource Programs piloted by HEW in the 1970s. Research
  consistently shows that violent crime is associated with
  childhood experiences in abusive or highly stressed families.

° States should help establish, fund and provide technical
  assistance to family violence reduction programs both within
  and outside of local criminal justice systems. Seventeen
  percent of homicides in 1981 involved family relationships;
  half of them were spouse killings.

Programs for Offenders

° States should develop programs to provide adequate financial
  assistance to released prisoners. Experiments in Maryland,
  Georgia, Texas and California have shown that post-release
  stipends can have a major impact on recidivism, for violent
  as well as property crimes.

° States should develop "supported work" programs as a community
  alternative to incarceration for many minor, especially non-
  violent offenders. These programs, pioneered in New York
  by the Vera Foundation, offer a carefully structured work
  program with gradually increasing rewards and responsibilities
  and a variety of support services. Careful evaluations
  suggest that they may be an especially effective approach for
  addicted criminals.

FOR FURTHER INFORMATION

Publications

American Prisons and Jails, Joan Mullen, et al, 1980.
U.S. Department of Justice, National Institute of Justice,
Washington, D.C. A thorough analysis of trends in imprisonment
and the options for reducing prison crowding.

Citizen Crime Prevention Tactics: A Literature Review
and Selected Bibliography, U.S. Department of Justice, National
Institute of Justice, Washington, D.C., 1980. Useful review of
various kinds of locally-based prevention programs and studies
of their effectiveness.

Court Reform on Trial, Malcolm Feeley, Basic Books, New
York, 1982. Important critique of several (not very successful)
efforts to reduce crime by "reforming" the courts.

Deterrence and Incapacitation: Estimating the Effects of
Criminal Sanctions on Crime Rates, Alfred Blumstein, Jacqueline
Cohen, and Daniel Nagin; National Academy of Sciences, Washington,
D.C., 1978. Technical, but extremely important, analyses of
the effects of increasing crime's "costs."

Summary and Findings of the National Supported Work
Demonstration, Manpower Demonstration Research Corporation,
Cambrige, MA, Ballinger Press, 1980. Careful description and
analysis of supported work experiments.

Organizations

CALIFORNIA COMMISSION ON CRIME CONTROL AND VIOLENCE PREVENTION,
9719 Lincoln Village Drive, Suite 600, Sacramento, CA 95827
(916) 366-5338. An example of a state-level research and advocacy
commission. Has published a report, Ounces of Prevention,
examining literature on causes and prevention of crime.

NATIONAL COUNCIL ON CRIME AND DELINQUENCY, Continental Plaza,
411 Hackensack Avenue, Hackensack, NJ 07601 (201) 488-0400.
National organization of concerned criminal justice profes-
sionals, researchers and citizens. Publishes a journal,
Crime and Delinquency, as well as quarterly Criminal Justice
Abstracts.

NATIONAL MORATORIUM ON PRISON CONSTRUCTION, Unitarian Univers-
alist Service Committee, 1251 Second Avenue, San Francisco, CA
94122 (415) 731-3300. Provides information on problems and
costs of incarceration and on alternatives to imprisonment.

Prepared by Elliott Currie.

Handgun Control

The statistics of handgun violence in America are appalling. In 1981, 11,258 Americans were murdered with handguns, 2.5 times more often than with any other weapon. That figure represents 50 percent of all the murders in America that year.

On an average day, 31 Americans are murdered with handguns. One in nine Americans has been threatened or attacked by someone wielding a handgun.

In 1981, 55 percent of handgun murders were perpetrated by relatives or persons acquainted with their victims. Of these murders, 17 percent were within families, half of which involved spouse killing spouse.

There are an estimated 55 million handguns in America, and every year almost 2.5 million new handguns are put into circulation. At the current rate of production, the American handgun population will be 100 million by the year 2000.

During the Vietnam War, more than 50,000 American soldiers were killed in action. During that same period, more than 50,000 Americans were murdered in the United States with handguns.

Because of its concealable and lethal nature, the handgun is the favorite weapon of criminals. According to the FBI statistics, handguns in 1981 were used in some 220,000 robberies and 154,000 aggravated assaults.

In 1980, handguns were used to kill eight people in Great Britain, 24 in Switzerland, eight in Canada, 23 in Israel, 18 in Sweden, four in Australia and 11,522 in the United States. Unlike the United States, these other Western nations have tough handgun control laws.

More important than the statistics on handgun violence are the lives they represent. "The victims of the violence are black and white, rich and poor, young and old, famous and unknown," said Robert Kennedy in 1968, just two months before he himself was to become a victim of handgun violence. "They are most important of all, human beings whom other human beings loved and needed. No one -- no matter where he lives or what he does -- can be certain who next will suffer from some senseless act of bloodshed. And yet it goes on and on in this country of ours. Why?"

THE PROBLEM

Six major arguments are made by the gun lobby in opposition to handgun control legislation:

"The Second Amendment guarantees individuals the right to keep and bear arms." In fact, the Second Amendment to the U.S. Constitution does not guarantee such a right to individuals. The Second Amendment reads in full: "A Well Regulated Militia Being Necessary to the Security of a Free State, the Right of the People to Keep and Bear Arms Shall Not Be Infringed."

On five separate occasions, the U.S. Supreme Court has ruled that the Second Amendment was intended to protect members of a state militia from being disarmed by the federal government. In addition, the American Bar Association has stated that "every Federal Court decision involving the amendment has given the amendment a collective, militia interpretation and/or held that firearms control laws enacted under a state's police power are constitutional."

There recently have been three significant court decisions upholding the rights of states and localities to control handguns. The Ohio Supreme Court has upheld one community's laws requiring a special weapon owners' identification card; and the U.S. District Court has ruled the Morton Grove, Illinois restrictive handgun ordinance is constitutional. A Rhode Island law requiring handgun purchasers to obtain a safety certificate has been upheld by the U.S. District Court as a reasonable way to promote handgun safety.

"Gun control will leave citizens defenseless from criminals." Under federal legislation proposed by Senator Edward Kennedy and Congressman Peter Rodino (the Kennedy-Rodino Handgun Crime Control Bill), law-abiding citizens will still have no difficulty getting handguns. Even so, citizens should think twice before getting a handgun for self-protection.

Statistics show clearly that a handgun kept for self-defense is far more dangerous to its owner and his family than it is to the criminal. For example, California statistics show that if you purchase a gun it is over 11 times as likely to be used to kill you, your spouse or your children as it is to kill an intruder in your home.

"When guns are outlawed, only outlaws will have guns." This is one of the simplest -- and most popular -- slogans of the gun lobby. Under any realistic federal control of handguns (such as the Kennedy-Rodino Bill), law-abiding citizens will still be able to buy handguns, but it will be more difficult for criminals to get them. Furthermore, rifles and shotguns will not be affected at all by any handgun control legislation.

"Handgun control is the first step toward confiscation of all guns." Public opinion polls show what type of handgun control the American people want. A July, 1981 Gallup poll showed that 91 percent of the American people favor a three-week waiting period with a background check for handgun purchases. Handgun control is just handgun control -- not rifle control or shotgun control.

The United States is a democratic nation and under the democratic process laws will be passed to give the American people what they want, not what they don't want. Those in the gun lobby who compare the United States to Hitler's Germany or Communist regimes apparently have little faith in our democratic system.

"Guns don't kill, people do." People do kill people, but they do so mostly with handguns. The handgun is a weapon designed and made for the purpose of killing human beings and it is more lethal than any other murder weapon. It is used 2 1/2 times more often than any other murder weapon.

"People also kill people with automobiles," Pete Shields, Chairman of Handgun Control, Inc. recently wrote, "and thus we regulate their use, but the many local, state, and national car clubs do not bombard Congress and the public with appeals for the unregulated use of cars and trucks."

We regulate all kinds of other dangerous substances in our country. Drugs, for example, are strictly regulated, and those who dispense them must be licensed. Some drugs, such as heroin, are considered so lethal that they are banned entirely.

"Control criminals, not guns." It is true that we should do something to control criminals -- and one way is by controlling handguns, the criminal's favorite weapon. Admittedly, there are other things which need to be done to improve our criminal justice system -- prison reform and rehabilitation, judicial sentencing and parole, and a host of other solutions. We should put the criminals behind bars, but while we're doing that, we should also take preventive measures.

Handgun control is one way to make it more difficult for criminals to get their favorite tool -- the deadly, concealable handgun.

WHAT STATES CAN DO

States should enact handgun control laws based on one of the three following models:

Mandatory Sentences for Carrying Unlicensed Handguns

A Massachusetts law passed in 1975 is the toughest handgun control law in the country. Called the Bartley-Fox law, it requires a one-year mandatory minimum prison term for anyone caught carrying a handgun without a license outside his home or place of business.

Not only is the law tough, but effective. A study of the law's impact by the Center for Applied Social Research at Northeastern University in Boston showed that between 1974 and 1976, gun homicides in Boston declined 43 percent compared to 11.1 percent for other cities of similar size; gun-related armed robberies dropped 35.1 percent in Massachusetts compared to 11.7 percent in the rest of the country; and gun assaults declined by 19.3 percent in Massachusetts while dropping only 4.2 percent in the rest of the country.

Registration of Firearms and Freezing Handgun Sales

A 1977 District of Columbia law requires the registration of all currently owned handguns, rifles and shotguns and froze the number of legal handguns by banning the sale or possession of additional handguns by private citizens. A study of that law by Edward D. Jones III, a former analyst for the Justice Department, compared statistics in the District of Columbia for 1974 and 1978 (the first full year after the law went into effect) which showed that family killings caused by handgun abuse decreased from 10 percent in 1974 to five percent in 1978 and handgun homicides among neighbors, lovers and other nonfamily acquaintances dropped from 44 percent to 38 percent.

Mandatory Safety Course for Handgun Purchases

A Rhode Island law which took effect in 1980 requires handgun purchasers to take a four to six hour handgun safety course given by the Department of Environmental Management (DEM). If someone feels he does not need to take the course, he can take a test based on a DEM handgun safety manual. A certificate from the DEM certifying that the purchaser has completed the handgun safety course is required for purchasing a handgun.

FOR FURTHER INFORMATION

Publications

Guns Don't Die, People Do, by Pete Shields, Chairman of Handgun Control, Inc. Available at your local bookstore or order for $6.95 (price includes postage and handling) from Arbor House Publishing Company, 235 E. 45th St., New York, NY, 10017. This recently published book presents the case for handgun control, including an explanation of current gun laws and legislation before Congress. It provides shocking facts about handguns and what can and must be done about them.

Federal Regulation of Firearms, a report prepared by the Congressional Research Service of the Library of Congress for the Senate Judiciary Committee. Available for sale from the Superintendent of Documents, U.S. Government Printing Office, Washington, D.C. 20402. This government document provides a summation of major congressional legislation and of state handgun control laws.

"Second Amendment Symposium: Rights in Conflict in the 1980's," Northern Kentucky Law Review, Vol. 10, No. 1, 1982.

The Snub-Nosed Killers: Handguns in America, a series of articles which appeared in the Cox newspapers in fall 1981. This award-winning series presents evidence that handguns with a barrel-length of three inches or less are the most favored weapons of criminals.

Organizations

HANDGUN CONTROL, INC., 810 18th Street, N.W., Washington, D.C. 20006 (202) 638-4723. Works with state and local handgun control groups; will provide information on how to contact a group in your state or community.

NATIONAL COALITION TO BAN HANDGUNS, 100 Maryland Avenue, N.E., Washington, D.C. 20002 (202) 544-7190.

Prepared by Donald Fraher.

The Governmental Process

Block Grants

One of the most important issues confronting state and local governments in the 1980s is the federal block grant program.

The 1981 Omnibus Budget Reconciliation Act restructured many of the financial and programmatic relationships between the federal government and the states, consolidating 57 federal categorical aid programs into nine block grants.

Consolidation of categorical grants is only part of the Reagan administration's plan to cut back federal assistance to states and cities. When Reagan handed the states the nine block grants, he also reduced funding for these programs by 25 percent. Colorado Governor Richard Lamm recently observed that block grants in their current form are actually "more authority to do less."

For example, although grants to state and local government account for only 10.7 percent of the total federal budget for FY 1983, they account for 26.3 percent of the proposed budget cuts. These FY 1983 cuts come on top of equally severe budget cuts in these same grants in FY 1982.

Needy citizens suffer most from Reagan's turn-back and cut-back approach to human service programs. Of the more than $35 billion cut, more than $10 billion fell on families with incomes below $10,000 a year.

States have been put into a disastrous financial bind by the Reagan budgets. Most states must choose either to raise taxes to make up for federal cutbacks or to cut services. An Associated Press survey in 1982 of the 50 states found that:

° Eighteen states have cut spending and/or raised taxes or settled for deficits exceeding $30 million, or are facing such choices;

° Twenty states raised existing taxes or imposed new ones;

° Twenty states have laid off employees or stopped replacing those who leave. At least five states also delayed or rejected raises for state workers.

THE PROBLEM

One of the major sources of funds for state and local governments in the 1980s will be the federal government. Although President Reagan is dramatically cutting the amount of federal grants available to states and cities, federal money will continue to play a critical role in the financing of programs administered by states and cities.

Over the past two decades Congress successfully, but with great resistance, wrote important protections for the disadvantaged into federal categorical grant programs to the states. Strong lobbying by liberal, civil rights, client groups and others created strong protections to ensure that federal funds were used for the purposes Congress originally intended.

Protections written into the federal categorical grant programs included: 1) standards requiring public hearings and public participation in state decision making on federally-financed programs; 2) standard guidelines for regular evaluation of decision making; 3) regulations requiring state and local governmental compliance with civil rights law, accompanied by strong enforcement mechanisms; and 4) targeting of federally-financed programs to people most in need.

The Budget and Reconciliation Act of 1981 pushed through Congress by President Reagan and the conservative Republican/Democrat coalition substantially weakened the protections added by Congress. The federal guidelines covering the Reagan "block grants" are considerably weaker than the Congressional guidelines that had previously covered the federal categorical grant programs.

Further pressure to weaken the federal guidelines is strengthened by the combined effects of the recession and the massive cutbacks in the amount of federal funds delivered to states and cities. States are tempted to view block grant funds as an extension of general revenue sharing funds, and thus use them for purposes that are only remotely related to the specific purposes of the block grant programs.

In the face of the continually-weakened federal guidelines action by state governments is critical. New state
legislation is needed which incorporates progressive guidelines
and standards similar to those that passed in the 1960s and
1970s.

This action is needed in four interrelated areas involving
the nine Reagan-created federal block grant programs. These
four include:

Public Participation. Federal guidelines in the Budget
and Reconciliation Act of 1981 for public hearings and public
participation are extremely weak. Timely notice, wide publi-
city and accessible meetings are important elements of public
hearings. Most states complied with federal guidelines by
holding a single one-day hearing, covering all block grants.
One-fourth provided an opportunity for local governments,
agencies and public interest groups to participate.

Evaluation and Accountability. New federal guidelines
do not require sufficient data collection and reporting to
permit effective evaluation either by the states or by the
federal government. State data collection has been poor in
the past. Because of the lack of accurate and sufficient
data, it will be impossible to trace the expenditure of
funds and to evaluate their impact.

Civil Rights Compliance. While each of the block grants
do contain "boilerplate" civil rights language, they do not
include any particular enforcement mechanism either for the
federal government or individual citizens in ensuring that
federal funds are spent in a non-discriminatory manner.
Requiring adherence to civil rights law is meaningless without
strong enforcement mechanisms built into the law.

Targeting Services to Needy Citizens. There is considerable danger that federal grants programs that were targeted
to needy citizens will disappear as state budget deficits
increase. The pressure on legislatures by politically
powerful constituencies to use federal block grant funds for
their own purposes is already considerable. Block grant
funds may be shifted away from specific program areas to more
general ones, from the poorest recipients and low-income
communities to more politically powerful ones, out of small-
scale, community-based systems to larger, more established
delivery systems.

WHAT STATES CAN DO

Public Participation

° States should create Block Grant Advisory Commissions to
ensure public representation. They should include citizens
directly affected by programs, nonprofit agencies serving
principal beneficiaries and state officials.

° States should be required to give adequate notice of public
hearings on expenditure plans for block grants. The
hearings should encourage active debate among citizens.

Evaluation and Accountability

° States should enact legislation providing for systematic
data collection, accountability and evaluation of block
grant expenditures.

° States should enact legislation ensuring that citizens
will have access to the information needed to monitor and
assess the state's plans and performances.

° States should enact legislation that provides for an evaluation of performance by local citizens. The evaluation
should include a review of each project funded under the
categorical programs and a determination as to whether
they merit continued support.

Civil Rights Compliance

° States should enact legislation prohibiting discrimination.
This provision should assure that no person will be discriminated against on the grounds of sex, religion, race,
ethnic background, age or disability under any program
funded in whole or in part by federal block grant funds.

° States should enact legislation creating grievance procedures
for the principal beneficiaries of block grant funds.
Complaint hearings should be held before either an independent panel of citizens or a board of legislators.

Targeting Services to Needy Citizens

° States should enact legislation to ensure that the principal
beneficiaries of these block grant programs are individuals
in greatest need by reason of economic position, health,
age, family circumstances or disabled condition.

° States should enact legislation requiring that data be
collected to document the distribution of funds and program
services to targeted populations.

FOR FURTHER INFORMATION

Publications

Block Grants: A New Chance for State Legislatures to Oversee Federal Funds. Available from the National Conference of State Legislatures, Fiscal Affairs Program.

The Block Grant Briefing Book, Coalition on Block Grants and Human Needs, 1982.

The Challenge of Block Grants: States Implement CSBG. Available from the Institute for Local Self-Government, Hotel Claremont Building, Berkeley, CA 94705.

A Children's Defense Budget: An Analysis of the President's Budget and Children, Children's Defense Fund, 122 C Street, N.W., Washington, D.C. 20001 (202) 628-8787.

Florida's Implementation of Federal Block Grants. Available from the Florida Advisory Council of Intergovernmental Relations, Lewis State Office Building, Suite 400, Tallahassee, FL 32304.

Preserving Community Development Block Grant Standards: A Model City Council Resolution from Albuquerque, NM, $2.50 from the Conference on Alternative State and Local Policies, 2000 Florida Avenue, N.W., Washington, D.C. 20009.

Primer on Block Grants, Janet Schroyer-Portillo, National Council of La Raza, 1725 I Street, N.W., Washington, D.C. 20006 (202) 293-4680.

Summary and Comparison of the Legislative Provisions of the Block Grants Created by the 1981 Omnibus Budget Reconciliation Act, December 1982. General Accounting Office, Document Services, P.O. Box 6015, Gaithersburg, MD 20760. Document #IPE-83-2.

Organizations

CENTER ON BUDGET AND POLICY PRIORITIES, 236 Massachusetts Avenue, N.E., Room 305, Washington, D.C. 20002.

COALITION ON BLOCK GRANTS AND HUMAN NEEDS, 1000 Wisconsin Avenue, N.W., Washington, D.C. 20007 (202) 333-0822. Provides information on state and federal block grant coalitions.

NATIONAL CONFERENCE OF STATE LEGISLATURES, Fiscal Affairs Program, 1125 17th Street, Denver, C.O. 80202 (303) 623-6600.

NATIONAL GOVERNOR'S ASSOCIATION, 444 N. Capitol St., Washington, D.C. 20001 (202) 624-5300.

Prepared by Barbara Pape.

Corruption and Waste

<u>BACKGROUND FACTS</u>

One of the biggest concerns of American voters is governmental responsiveness and effectiveness. This issue is likely to continue to rank high on the voter's mind in the years ahead.

Numerous polls indicate that the overwhelming majority of citizens are suspicious of government at all levels. They believe that corruption is widespread, that fraud and waste in government programs are common and that government programs and policies frequently do not achieve their intended result.

In 1978, for example, the Harris survey reported that 84 percent of all citizens believed that corruption and payoffs were common. Those results are consistent with previous polls.

Four years earlier the Harris survey determined that 60 percent of the respondents felt that local government corruption was a serious problem. In a Roper poll that same year, 58 percent of those surveyed said that most or many people in government took payoffs.

Other polls have found that citizens simply do not believe that government is competent -- that it can't solve the problems the nation faces. In 1976, for example, President Carter's pollster Patrick Caddell found that only 10 percent to 13 percent of all citizens believed that government "will actually be able to do" something about the nation's most pressing problems.

Unfortunately, the public's perceptions, while perhaps exaggerated, do have a strong basis in fact. Public corruption, while difficult to measure, appears to be widespread. A National Institute of Justice survey of the nation's newpapers has indicated that reports of official corruption can be found throughout the country. While most cases of reported corruptions came from cities (53 percent), suburbs and counties were not far behind (42 percent).

Federal prosecutions of public officials, another measure of the extent of public corruption, have increased substantially over the past ten years. The Justice Department's Public Integrity Section reports that 211 local officials were convicted for federal crimes in 1981, up from 16 convictions in 1970. Last year 3,937 federal, state and local officials were convicted by federal prosecutors.

In dollar terms, the results of fraud and waste are staggering. In the late 1970s, Attorney General Benjamin Civiletti estimated that the government lost between $2.5 and $25 billion each year through fraud.

THE PROBLEM

Throughout the past decade there has been a steady erosion of the public's confidence in its major institutions. Government officials face especially difficult problems in overcoming citizens' skepticism in the post-Watergate era. Public opinion polls repeatedly reflect the widespread perception that official corruption is pervasive. Furthermore, government programs to help the poor or assist in economic development are often viewed as being riddled with fraud.

Progressives have been outspoken advocates of more open government. They have led reform drives in many states to enact campaign election laws, provide for financial disclosure by public officials and pass open meetings legislation. These reforms are, in part, designed to deter official corruption which thrives on secrecy. Yet, generally, issues concerning fraud and waste in government programs have not been high on the list of progressive issues. Both official corruption and program abuse, especially abuse by service providers, are important problems that have contributed to the crisis of confidence that affects government. It is essential that those who design and support the goals of many government social programs take an active role in preserving the integrity of these programs.

Public corruption not only destroys citizens' faith in government, but also creates bitterness about their wasted tax dollars. Public corruption imposes a direct cost on taxpayers. Bid-rigging schemes raise the price of public contracts and can lead to an increase in taxes. A bribe to obtain a zoning variance -- from lower to higher population density, for example -- could mean that high-rise buildings are built where they do not belong. Schools become overcrowded, highways more congested and the general quality of life diminishes. And taxpayers pay the bill.

Corruption, of course, cannot be eliminated from public life. However, there are practical steps that government officials can take to deter public corruption and protect the integrity of government programs. One approach is designed to enhance government accountability by opening government decision-making to public scrutiny -- for example, campaign finance and financial disclosure laws. A second strategy involves implementing specific measures to reduce fraud, waste and abuse in goverment programs. This approach emphasizes the steps that can be taken to detect, investigate and prevent fraud and waste in goverment programs, such as by establishing Inspectors General (IGs) in agencies.

Over the past few years many states have enacted legislation in the areas of campaign finance, conflict of interest regulation and requiring open meetings.

Common Cause reports that there are now 47 states that require candidates to file disclosure reports before elections. Individual contribution limits are in effect in 23 states. Seventeen states have enacted public financing for state elections.

In the area of conflict of interest regulation, 44 states now require some form of financial disclosure by public officials. Independent ethics commissions monitor and enforce those disclosure laws in 31 states.

All states now have open meetings laws and 45 states have strengthened their laws over the past decade. Sanctions for violating the open meetings laws are provided in 36 states.

Borrowing from the federal model, some states have created Inspectors General (IGs) to coordinate efforts to prevent fraud and waste. The use of "hotlines" provides a means by which the public can report instances of program abuse. Vulnerability Assessment has proven effective at the federal level. This approach assesses a program's vulnerability to waste and fraud, emphasizing prevention rather than investigation and detection.

Several arguments have been made against various open government reforms. Campaign finance reforms that restrict individual contributions, for example, have been attacked on First Amendment grounds. Additionally, financial disclosure has been challenged as an invasion of a public official's privacy and on the basis that they would deter well-qualified persons from seeking public office.

According to Common Cause, virtually all state courts that have considered personal financial disclosure laws for public officials have upheld their legality. Generally, they have reasoned that the public's right to know outweighs the need for privacy if the disclosure laws do not unduly intrude into intimate personal matters.

There is little evidence that such laws deter many well-qualified applicants from seeking office. Washington state, for example, enacted a disclosure law in 1972 covering 272 elected state officials. Only one resignation has been attributed to the laws.

WHAT STATES CAN DO

Open and Accountable Government

° States should pass legislation to require public financing of state elections. Seventeen states have already passed such legislation.

° States should, as a part of public financing, restrict the total amount of campaign expenditures and the total amount of money that a candidate can receive from political action committees.

° States should require quarterly reporting of all contributions to political candidates based on the guidelines used by the Federal Election Commission.

° States should require the disclosure of personal and business finances for all candidates for elected office and nominees for major appointed office. In addition, states should require incumbent public officials and major administrators to file these reports at least once a year.

° States should strengthen or if necessary, pass legislation to ensure the public's right of access to government records. The federal law provides a reasonably good model for state legislation.

° States should enact legislation to protect public employee whistle-blowers from reprisals. Michigan forbids employers from discriminating against, threatening or firing employees who report or plan to report violations of federal, state or local laws.

Program Integrity

° States should enact legislation to establish state Inspector General offices based on the federal model. These officials should be politically independent (for example, dismissed only by the state's top executive) and have subpoena power. Massachusetts and New York have established IG's through legislation, although the IG's jurisdiction is limited.

° States should establish hotlines which allow citizens and state employees to disclose instances of program abuse. California, Washington and South Carolina use such hotlines. The California hotline is primarily designed to allow state employees to disclose improper governmental activities.

° States should enact legislation allowing individual lawsuits against fraud and waste. This would permit individual taxpayers to sue for the recovery of money for the government when official enforcement is lax or inadequate.

FOR FURTHER INFORMATION

Publications

Anticorruption Strategy For Local Governments, T. Fletcher, et al., Stanford Research Institute, Menlo Park, California, 1979.

Campaign Finance Reform and the States, Conference on Alternative State and Local Policies, 1983. 2000 Florida Avenue N.W., Washington, D.C. 20009.

Fraud in Government Benefit Programs, J.A. Gardiner, et al., National Institute of Justice, U.S. Department of Justice, 1982.

Maintaining Municipal Integrity: Trainers Handbook, D. Austern, et al., National Institute of Justice, U.S. Department of Justice, 1980. Contains model legislation in the areas of conflicts of interest, public contracting, open meetings and the protection of public employees from retaliation.

Public Financing of State Elections, Herbert E. Alexander and Jennifer W. Frutig, Citizens' Research Foundation, University of Southern California, 1982. An election guide to public funding of political parties and candidates in 17 states.

Organizations

BETTER GOVERNMENT ASSOCIATION (BGA), 1901 Pennsylvania Avenue, N.W., Washington, D.C., 20006 (202) 223-6164; and 230 N. Michigan Ave., Chicago, IL, 60601, (312) 641-1181. The BGA conducts investigations and publishes reports on governmental performance.

COMMON CAUSE, 2030 M Street, N.W., Washington, D.C. 20036 (202) 833-1200. State Common Cause offices are listed in the state capital telephone directory.

LEAGUE OF WOMEN VOTERS, 1730 M Street, N.W., Washington, D.C. 20036 (202) 296-1770.

NATIONAL ASSOCIATION OF STATE AUDITORS, COMPTROLLERS AND TREASURERS, 444 N. Capitol Street, N.W., Suite 240, Washington, D.C. 20001 (202) 624-5451.

PUBLIC CITIZEN LITIGATION GROUP, 2000 P Street, N.W., Suite 700, Washington, D.C., 20036. Has model state Freedom of Information legislation.

Prepared by Peter Manikas.

Consumer Issues

Consumer Protection

BACKGROUND FACTS

Consumers cannot count on the federal government for protection.

The Reagan policy now focuses on protection of the producer. The clear assumption is that the marketplace will protect the consumer.

The high cost of credit has led to a tremendous rise in costs of consumer goods. In larger states, it is estimated that every percentage increase in interest rates translates into $100 million in increased costs to consumers.

Homeownership is available to only about five percent of those who do not already own a home. Five years ago it was normal and expected for housing costs to be about 25 percent of a family's disposable income. Housing now takes up 50 percent of disposable income for millions of families.

Health care costs have increased more than one and a half times the inflation rate. And despite huge outlays for medical care, the U.S. has the 13th highest infant mortality rate in the world.

High energy costs force up all other costs for consumers. Utility rates have more than tripled in the last five years. For many, utility bills exceed mortgage bills. The federal government has radically reduced its investment in conservation and development of alternative energy technologies.

And as a result of the AT&T break-up, approved by the Reagan administration, the telephone bills of most residential customers will more than double, while the bills of large businesses will decrease substantially.

Budget pressures at the federal level, coupled with the Reagan administration's opposition to consumer protection have decimated public complaint-handling agencies. The FTC, the FDA, the CPSC, the NHTSA, the FCC, the Department of Justice and other federal regulatory agencies for consumer protection have all suffered substantial funding losses.

THE PROBLEM

Consumers are "protected" by themselves, by advocates, and by government. To the extent that individual and collective consumer self-help is possible the consumer is stronger.

But reliance upon a self-regulating market cannot take care of consumer protection: public policies and programs are essential.

Consumers have not been able recently to focus their power. The current problems of our economy, skepticism about the effectiveness of government, and the lack of public access to corporate information have weakened consumer movements. And most consumer "problems" present themselves in such ad hoc or episodic fashion that sustained interest is often difficult for many people.

The questions become, how do we empower consumers for "self-protection" and how do we "protect" consumers where the task is beyond the private state of the art?

Self Protection: Information is obviously essential. Intelligible market information, practical how-to manuals, travel guides to the public "procedures," and other such resources are indispensable tools. There is a plethora of information; the task is one of locating it, translating it and making it available. Information can assist the individual consumer in becoming aware and avoiding victimization, in recognizing and getting maximum quality in goods and services, in becoming a smart marketplace actor and in securing redress.

Organization for collective action also expands the power of the consumer. Organized action permits specific consumer problems to be solved and equips individuals pitted against organized market and governmental forces with the resources needed to launch and win an effective consumer campaign.

Cooperatives, one form of consumer group, well illustrate the advantages of organization. Co-ops save people money, provide a network for the dissemination of consumer information, and may become the base for other consumer interest activity.

Utility rates, energy conservation and alternative energy development are among fundamental consumer issues that can be addressed by another form of consumer organization, such as a Consumers Utility Board (CUB). A CUB is a voluntary, nonprofit membership organization enabled by a state legislature and funded by ratepayers through the utility billing system. These organizations, staffed by specialists, represent ratepayers' interests in rate-setting and broader energy policy proceedings.

Other consumer groups are organized around auto repair, complaint mediation, health care, prenatal services, nutrition, owner-building, money-lending, campus issues, insurance abuses and so on. Very effective consumer action can be developed in already existing affinity groups such as neighborhood, church, ethnic, or senior citizen organizations. The key is identification of concerns that will attract many consumers to participate in a united endeavor.

Public Participation Protection: Consumers can exercise significant power through membership on public advisory boards and regulatory bodies. For example, professional and occupational licensing boards regulate millions of purveyors of consumer goods and services. A recent movement seeks to place "public" members on such boards, often as majorities, as in California. This sort of participation in governance can lead to real consumer self-determination.

Public Consumer Protection: Some areas of consumer problems require public regulation, because their scope extends well beyond the range of actions that individuals or groups can take to protect themselves.

Among others, this category includes food and drug safety, auto and highway safety, money and credit practices, and marketplace competition. But distinct policies mandating regulation in one area and not in another exist. And so consumer groups are often involved -- and needed -- at all levels.

Some state consumer protection agencies have performed most admirably. Depending on state statute, their powers can include litigation, research, complaint-handling, consumer education, legislative and administrative advocacy and technical assistance (for example, on co-op formation). Such functions supplement private consumer action and bring together an expertise and pool of financial resources that would otherwise be very difficult to acquire. In policy-making forums the presence of a state consumer agency -- especially if it has public and private consumer group support -- can be wonderfully galvanizing.

Another key public consumer protection function is the complaint-handling agency. When consumer complaints against businesses can be resolved expeditiously, the economic and social climate of a local community is strengthened.

Small claims court is already an effective public consumer protection agency. Further innovations, such as raising the dollar limit, holding night and weekend sessions and making translators and advisors available, could solidify this institution's reputation as a source of redress and protection.

WHAT STATES CAN DO

Consumer Protection Agency

° States should establish a strong consumer protection agency,
  with a broad range of advocacy, education, research, mediation and assistance powers. A consumer agency should be
  encouraged to develop and work closely with consumers to
  ensure both accountability and effectiveness.

Consumer Representation

° States should establish a Consumers Utility Board to represent consumers in agency and judicial proceedings, lobby for
  consumer interests and provide consumers with information.

° States should put a majority of "public members" on regulatory advisory bodies, especially professional licensing
  bodies and agricultural marketing boards. California has
  already done this most successfully and other states are
  beginning to follow suit.

° States should encourage development of consumer cooperatives,
  such as California's Cooperative Development Program or
  Wisconsin's University Center for Cooperatives.

Legal Relief

° States should reform the small claims court process to
  make it more a people's court. New York has enacted several
  small claims court reform laws, as have California and
  Massachusetts.

° States should provide by statute for attorney's fees for
  successful litigants in consumer cases. This "private
  attorney general" approach is well-founded in legal tradition
  and established by laws in several states.

° States should establish a network of community-based dispute
  resolution centers to mediate minor consumer disputes and
  other neighborhood tensions. (New York City has instituted
  such mediation centers.)

Other

° States should initiate a thorough review of health care
  systems to address appropriate use of technologies, more
  aggressive and less doctor-dominated health care personnel
  mixes for prevention and "wellness" programs and innovative
  cost control measures such as California's new Health Cost
  Czar.

FOR FURTHER INFORMATION

Publications

The Complete California Consumer Catalog, California Department of Consumer Affairs, $3.00. Award-winning how-to manual on scores of standard consumer problems.

A Model Act for a Residential Utility Consumer Action Group, available from The Center for the Study of Responsive Law, P.O. Box 19367, Washington, D.C. 20036.

The Record on Elected and Appointed Utility Commissions, A Public Action Report, available through the Illinois Public Action Council, 59 East Van Buren Street, Chicago, IL 60605.

Newsletter, Consumer Federation of America, 1314 14th Street N.W., Washington, D.C. 20005. The Federation has an extensive list of consumer publications.

Organizations

CALIFORNIA DEPARTMENT OF CONSUMER AFFAIRS, 1020 N Street, Sacramento, CA, 95814, (916) 445-4465. Wide range of programs.

CENTER FOR THE STUDY OF RESPONSIVE LAW, P.O. Box 19367, Washington, D.C. 20036. A Ralph Nader group, providing technical assistance and resources materials for consumer group issues and organizing. Does some state and national networking.

CONSUMER EDUCATION RESOURCE NETWORK (C.E.R.N.), 1500 Wilson Blvd., Rosslyn, VA 22209. Excellent bibliographic services. For specific issues, CERN is the best single source of assistance.

CONSUMER FEDERATION OF AMERICA, 1314 14th Street, N.W., #901, Washington, D.C. 20005. Provides information and networking for national, state and local consumer groups.

CONSUMERS UNION, 256 Washington Street, Mt. Vernon, NY, 10550. National membership organization, with regional offices and education, litigation and advocacy programs.

NATIONAL ASSOCIATION OF CONSUMER AGENCY ADMINISTRATORS, 1511 K Street, N.W., Washington, D.C. 20005. Provides networking for state and local public consumer agencies.

NATIONAL CENTER FOR THE STUDY OF PROFESSIONS, 1527 New Hampshire Avenue, N.W., Washington, D.C. 20036. Good newsletter and materials on reforming professional and occupational licensing processes.

Prepared by Richard Spohn.

Insurance

Insurance company assets are 750 billion dollars or 2.5 times the assets of the oil companies.

The major insurance companies are among the largest corporations in the United States. In 1979, the industry employed more than 1.7 million workers.

This enormous industry, on average, represents an expenditure of over $1,300 for every man, woman and child in the country. Fully 12 percent of the nation's disposable income goes into insurance premiums.

States have nearly sole power to regulate the insurance industry. In 1945, following heavy insurer lobbying, Congress delegated regulation responsibility to the states with no standards for state law or enforcement.

In general, states' regulatory performance has been inadequate. In 1979, the General Accounting Office (GAO) found "serious shortcomings in state laws and regulatory activities with respect to protecting the interests of insurance consumers in the United States," noting that "insurance regulation is not characterized by an arms-length relationship between the regulators and the regulated." (Emphasis added.)

The insurance industry is a major lobbyist. It is very effective in Washington D.C. and is unarguably, the largest single lobbying force at the state level. Millions of dollars are spent each year arguing for rate increases before state insurance commissioners and for and against bills in the state legislatures. These costs are passed on to the consumers.

In many lines of insurance, cartels still either set rates for the whole market or for large shares of the market. When they set rates, they set them at the level to keep their least efficient members profitable. Even when they don't set rates, trade associations make key actuarial judgements about future economic conditions, set classes and territories and substantially lessen the flow of competition.

Insurance abuses are all too common. The worst cases include sharp Medicare insurance salespersons who prey on the elderly, expensive industrial life insurance which is oversold to the poor, the redlining of neighborhoods and sex discrimination.

THE PROBLEM

The insurance industry is not truly competitive. If it were, consumers would be better off.

Competition is weakened by many factors, including complexity of the product, product differentiation and lack of full disclosure of needed information. These factors restrict competitive buying by the consumer, particularly for life insurance (where, for example, access to information concerning rates of return paid on the savings portion of their life policies is unavailable) and increases the likelihood of manipulation of the consumer and poor consumer judgement.

In many states competition is also restricted. Anti-rebate laws are one of the problems. These laws make unlawful the reduction by independent insurance agents of commission rates set by various insurance groups. The law's aim was to prevent dishonest agents from convincing the consumer to buy dubious policies by promising free gifts or rebates on the agent's commission -- commissions which, ranging from 30 percent to over 100 percent, encourage unscrupulous behavior and significantly raise consumer costs. The actual effect, however, is to stifle competition. Just as in the old "Fair Trade Law" days, the wholesalers (the insurers) set commissions so their least efficient retailer (agent) stays profitable.

The roots of the industry's inefficiency are manifold: price-fixing and the absence of accountability requirements (whether to stock-holders, consumers or often, state regulatory agencies) are two major causes. Because antitrust statutes largely exempt the insurance industry, motivation remains towards greater growth rather than toward a leaner, more streamlined operation. For many reasons, including concern for the profitability of these large employers, state regulators are anxious to keep even inefficient companies profitable. There is insufficient motivation to experiment, to innovate, to change.

While the interests of the insurance companies are well represented in the legislative and regulatory arenas, the consumer is not. The monolithic nature of the industry, the complexities of investigation and reform, and the prohibitive costs of retaining actuaries, lawyers and other staff have effectively limited consumer action.

The Federal Trade Commission (FTC) and the Federal Insurance Administration (FIA) had taken steps in the mid- to late-1970s to help consumers through publication of reports on life insurance costs, disclosure, redlining and other central insurance issues. Congress has moved, however, under insurance industry lobbying pressure, to deny FTC the authority even to study insurance. FIA has been restructured and has ended its pro-consumer activities.

Some states actively represent consumer interests. In New Jersey and South Carolina, the state legislatures created a separate state agency to intervene in insurance rate cases on behalf of consumers; and in Massachusetts, the Attorney General is a statutory intervenor on their behalf. In these three states, intervention by experts has demonstrably saved hundreds of millions of dollars for consumers.

In New Jersey, the function of representing the consumer in rate cases, court cases, and legislative matters has been given, by law, to the Department of Public Advocate. The costs of intervention -- such as the hiring of expert witnesses -- is passed back to the filing insurer. The system requires a decision by the Public Advocate on whether or not to intervene. All rate filings and other matters of interest are required to be sent to the Public Advocate for review. Once the Public Advocate intervenes, questions regarding the filing, issues raised by the matter and so on are presented to the insurance company, which must respond. Ultimately unless a settlement occurs, a hearing is held before the insurance commissioners, who later render a decision based on input from the insurer and the Public Advocate.

In South Carolina, the process is similar. The South Carolina Office of Consumer Advocate handles these matters. In South Carolina, one major difference is that funding for expert witnesses and the like is by appropriation.

In the area of public utilities, Wisconsin citizens formed a Citizens Utility Board (CUB) which represents residential consumers on utility issues before state regulatory agencies, the legislature and other branches of government. The funding of the CUB is voluntary and it receives no tax dollars. However, an important element of CUB's enabling legislation gives CUB the right to enclose notices in utility bills. This gives unorganized consumers the means to organize and protect themselves.

In insurance, a Citizens Insurance Board (CIB) would perform similar functions and additionally, would disseminate consumer information to help its members shop for insurance.

WHAT STATES CAN DO

Primary Need

° States should institutionalize consumer representation in administrative, legislative and judicial proceedings by establishing Consumer Insurance Boards. The CIB would be funded by voluntary contributions from consumers who would receive notice of the organization in their bills.

Consumer Responsiveness

° State insurance commissions should prepare consumer booklets, including names and rates of specific insurance companies and publish comparative price guides on various types of insurance including homeowner, automobile, life and others.

° State insurance commissions should create a toll-free line for consumer complaints; should provide follow-up and back up to consumer complaints vis a vis individual insurance companies; and should publish surveys comparing the record of individual insurance companies in handling complaints.

° State insurance commissions should require that insurance policies be written simply and clearly, in plain, non-technical language.

° State insurance commissions should develop regulations, like those of New York, that allow broad access to the election of Board of Directors and provide for greater stockholder and public participation in the decisions of the companies. Rival slates of directors should be given access to mailing lists and equivalent corporate support in mutual insurance elections.

Affirmative Action

° State insurance commissions should require insurance companies to develop affirmative action programs to promote women and minorities into more responsible and well-paid positions.

Economic Development

° States should enact legislation to create an insurance company-financed publicly chartered corporation, such as the Massachusetts Capital Resource Company, to provide loans to small businesses to create in-state jobs.

Health Costs

° State insurance commissions should require Blue Cross/Blue Shield to play a stronger role in controlling the costs of hospital and doctor services. Fee screens should be reintroduced in lieu of the "Usual and Customary" approach in order to hold down costs.

FOR FURTHER INFORMATION

Publications

The "Agent" and the "Arbiter:" Two Important Actors on the Regulatory Stage, Harvard Business School, 1981, Cambridge, Massachusetts.

Government Facilitation of Consumerism: A Proposal for Consumer Action Groups, Arthur Best and Bernard L. Brown, Temple Law Quarterly, Volume 50, 1977. (Particularly the section on Insurance and the Appendix -- An Act to Create an Insurance Consumer Action Group.)

The Invisible Bankers: Everything the Insurance Industry Never Wanted You To Know, Andrew Tobias, 1982, Linden Press, $15.50.

Issues and Needed Improvements in State Regulation of the Insurance Business, U.S. Government General Accounting Office, October 9, 1979, PAD-79-72, Box 6015, Gaithersburg, MD 20877 (202) 275-6241.

Organizations

CUB CAMPAIGN, P.O. Box 19312, Washington, D.C. 20036 (202) 387-8030. Works with the Wisconsin Citizens' Utility Board, provides information to people interested in CUBs, including copies of model legislation, fact sheets, etc.

NATIONAL INSURANCE CONSUMER ORGANIZATION, 344 Commerce Street, Alexandria, VA 22314 (703) 549-8050. Robert Hunter, President. Publishes consumer guides and represents consumers in state and federal insurance matters.

NEW JERSEY DEPARTMENT OF PUBLIC ADVOCATE, 520 E. State Street, P.O. Box 141, Trenton, NJ 08625.

SOUTH CAROLINA OFFICE OF CONSUMER ADVOCATE, Department of Consumer Affairs, 2221 Devine Street, P.O. Box 5757, Columbia, SC 20250.

Prepared by Robert Hunter.

Tax Reform

BACKGROUND FACTS

In seven of the eight years preceding Ronald Reagan's election to the Presidency, the net effect of state and local legislative actions on taxes was to cut taxes.

This has changed. In 1981 and 1982, more than half of the states raised one tax or another, adding $8 billion to the total state tax bill. This year, 43 states are considering bills that would boost collections by more than $12 billion annually. Cities and counties too have begun to raise property taxes and have begun to charge new or higher fees for the provisions of various services, ranging from sewage treatment to library cards.

It is no accident that this sharp reversal of trend coincides with the onset of the Reagan economic program. That program has put severe pressure on the financial security of state and local governments in four principal ways.

First, grants-in-aid to state and local governments have suffered more than their fair share of the Reagan budget cuts. Between 1982 and 1984, state and local governments will receive $48 billion less in federal assistance than they would have received under pre-Reagan policy.

Second, the recession, made more severe by Reagan's tax and spending policies, has caused dramatic reductions in tax collections and equally dramatic increases in claims on government services.

Third, the ill-named Economic Recovery Tax Act of 1981 (ERTA) contained a number of new tax-free investment vehicles. These tax giveaways have crowded-out the market for state and local bonds, driving up interest rates.

Fourth, Accelerated Cost Recovery System (ACRS), which will reduce federal business income tax collections by more than $120 billion between FY 83 and FY 87, can cause similar damage to state business tax revenues. If all states with corporate and personal income taxes were to conform to ACRS in its entirety -- even after the reforms adopted as part of the Tax Equity and Fiscal Responsibility Act of 1982 -- they would lose in excess of $17 billion over the next five fiscal years.

Given this context, states and cities have been forced to raise taxes -- and will continue to be forced to raise taxes. That much is clear. The only questions remaining to be resolved are "Which taxes?" and "Who will pay them?"

THE PROBLEM

The shift in funding responsibility away from the federal government toward state and local governments means a shift from a tax system based on a mildly progressive income tax to tax systems based on regressive sales and property taxes. But there are alternatives. Much can be done to restructure state and local tax systems to make them less regressive. In this way, both the fairness and the level of state and local taxes can be increased.

There are two major obstacles to this effort:

1. A widespread belief that the level of state and local taxes is a key determinant of business location decisions; and

2. Insensitivity to the issue of tax fairness on the part of progressives, citizens groups and labor organizations.

Business taxes are a critical element of any progressive tax system. Without them, most income generated from the ownership of capital, for example, stocks and bonds, would go untaxed. (And since the richer a person is, the greater is the proportion of his or her income that is "unearned," low business taxes mean a significant reduction in the overall tax burdens of the wealthy.)

This is only true, of course, if business taxes aren't "passed through" to consumers. The fact that business lobbyists become so enraged at the very mention of a business tax hike suggests that businesses don't possess the kind of ability to pass-through taxes as often as they would like. So does the fact that these same lobbyists never argue that lower business taxes might result in lower consumer prices.

More specifically, though, the ability of businesses to pass-through taxes is limited by the amount of competition facing a particular business and the number of substitutes for the product produced by a particular business. The greater the competition and the larger the number of substitutes, the less the ability to "pass-through" taxes. Even firms with substantial monopoly power will be limited in their ability to pass-through taxes, since they will have already pushed and probed the market to determine what price maximizes profits. A tax increase won't change this price.

Therefore, the owners of businesses -- shareholders, partners and sole proprietors -- ultimately bear the lion's share of the burden of business taxes. And only if this is true does the "business tax climate" argument make any sense at all.

Still, the notion that state and local taxes play a key role in the location decisions of businesses cannot stand up to scrutiny. State and local taxes make up only two to three percent of a business's total costs; interstate differences in the level of these taxes constitute only a small fraction of this two to three percent. Moreover, since state tax payments are deductible from federal tax liability, whatever difference in tax levels exists between states is automatically halved. Compared to interstate differences in labor or energy costs, interstate differences in the cost of state and local taxes are insignificant.

However, firms look at more than just the costs of doing business in different locations, they also look at the relative benefits of different sites. Among those benefits are things government provides -- good roads and bridges so that products can be transported efficiently, good schools so that workers are productive, good sewers, good police and fire protection, and so on. If states and localities do not have enough money to provide these services, then the relative attractiveness of their state or their locality will be diminished. Thus, by giving away their business tax bases, states and localities which have bought into the "business tax climate" view, may actually be losing their ability to provide those things which really are key determinants of business locations.

Finally, the positive obligation of businesses to help pay for government should be asserted. Justice Holmes once remarked, "Taxes are the price we pay for a civilized society." Certainly businesses are among the primary beneficiaries of civilized society. Our court system protects the rights of individuals to contract freely with one another and protects the inviolability of these contracts. Police and fire protection provide security from wanton attacks on private property. Highways and bridges allow the transport of goods between cities. Public schools provide the skilled labor force needed to keep our country competitive in international markets. In short, because businesses benefit from government services they should help pay for them.

The progressive political movement has failed to take seriously the issue of tax fairness for middle- and lower-income taxpayers. Focusing their attention exclusively on the expenditure side of federal, state and local budgets, progressives have permitted right-wing crusaders like Howard Jarvis and Jack Kemp to dominate public debate on taxes. Exploiting popular frustration with very real tax burdens, these individuals have successfully promoted legislation which has done very little to reduce the real tax burdens of the vast majority of Americans, but have very significantly slashed the taxes of the wealthiest individuals and corporations in this country.

WHAT STATES CAN DO

Business Taxation

° States should "decouple" from ACRS -- permanently. The
simplest way to "decouple" from ACRS revenue loss is to
require that businesses add-back for state income tax
purposes, a certain percentage of the ACRS deductions claimed
at the federal level. This step will prevent the elimination
of corporate income tax.

° States should adopt the "unitary worldwide combination"
system of reporting corporate profits. This would require
multi-state or multi-national corporations to report total
worldwide profits and pay taxes on the share proportionate
to the state's interest.

° States should stop tax abatements designed to promote
economic development, particularly in urban areas.

Income Taxation

° States should enact income taxes if they do not already
have them. These should be graduated taxes.

° States should give their counties and cities the authority
to enact graduated income taxes.

° States should exempt items from the sales tax such as
food, clothing and prescription drugs which are major
spending items for low- and moderate-income families.

Property Taxation

° States should enact property tax "circuit breakers," which
reimburse individuals whose property taxes exceed a certain
percentage of family income.

° States should enact metropolitan tax base sharing to allevi-
ate property tax disparities between cities and their
suburbs. Minnesota, for instance, has adopted a plan in
which 40 percent of any industrial or commercial growth in
certain metropolitan areas is shared by all the communities
in that area.

Other

° States should require the publication of a "Tax Expenditure
Budget" so that the revenue losses associated with the various
exemptions, preferences and loopholes built into the state
tax code may be readily known.

FOR FURTHER INFORMATION

Publications

How the States Can Respond to the 1981 Changes in Federal Depreciation Rules, 1981. Washington, D.C.: Citizens for Tax Justice.

Interstate Tax Competition, Advisory Commission on Intergovernmental Relations, Washington, D.C.

Natural Resource Taxation: Perspectives, Resources and Issues, 1980. Available from the Conference on Alternative State and Local Policies, $5.95.

Significant Features of Fiscal Federalism, 1981-82 Edition, Advisory Commission on Intergovernmental Relations, Washington, D.C.

State and Local Tax Reform: An Agenda for State and Local Governments, Lee Webb and David Wilhelm, 1982. A model agenda available from the Conference on Alternative State and Local Policies, $3.50.

State and Local Tax Revolt: New Directions for the '80s, edited by Dean Tipps and Lee Webb, 1981. Available from the Conference on Alternative State and Local Policies, $4.95.

State Taxation and Economic Development, Roger Vaughan, Council of State Planning Agencies, 400 N. Capitol Street, N.W., Washington, D.C. 20001.

Organizations

ADVISORY COMMISSION ON INTERGOVERNMENTAL RELATIONS, 1111 20th Street N.W., Washington, D.C. 20575 (202) 653-5540.

CITIZENS FOR TAX JUSTICE, 1825 K Street, N.W., Washington, D.C. 20006 (202) 293-5430.

FEDERATION OF TAX ADMINISTRATORS, 444 N. Capitol Street N.W., Suite 334, Washington, D.C. 20001 (202) 624-5890.

MULTISTATE TAX COMMISSION, 1790 30th Street, Boulder, CO 80301 (303) 447-9645. Eugene Corrigan, Executive Director.

NATIONAL CONFERENCE OF STATE LEGISLATURES, 1125 17th Street, Suite 1500, Denver, CO 80202 (303) 292-6600.

NATIONAL GOVERNORS ASSOCIATION, 444 N. Capitol Street N.W., Suite 250, Washington, D.C. 20001 (202) 624-5300.

Prepared by David Wilhelm.

Utilities

The price of electricity continues to rise. New records for cost per kilowatt are established each year.

The increase in the price of electricity has been far greater than the rate of inflation over the past decade. According to national averages, a kilowatt hour that sold for 1.67 cents in 1970 tripled in cost by 1982 and sold for 6.5 cents per kilowatt hour.

For most Americans, the increased price of electricity have been disastrous. For some, it has been fatal. In Huntsville, Alabama, eight people, including five small children, died in 1982 in a fire touched off by a lighted candle after the local utility shut the family's power off for non-payments. The New York Times estimated that so-called "terminations" took 200 lives in the last three years.

Due in part to generous rate increases, utility stocks are outperforming industrial stocks. In 1982, the total return on electric utility stocks was 35.4 percent compared with 20.2 percent for Standard & Poor's index of 400 industrial stocks.

To increase profit margins, a utility-sponsored group called the Committee for Energy Awareness has launched a $25 million a year advertising campaign designed to convince the public that more price increases are necessary in order for the industry to spend $35 billion a year through 1990 (and about $1 trillion by 2000) on the construction of new generating plants.

The problem with increasing the country's electric generating capacity is that the demand for electricity has plummeted. In 1982 the peak demand for electricity actually dropped 2.7 percent for the first time since 1945, leaving the utilities with an embarrassing 40 percent reserve margin. Fifteen percent is considered an adequate margin to ensure reliability. Even in the unlikely event that industry projections of 4 and 5 percent annual growth in sales prove true, the utilities' own figures indicate that reserve margins would hover around 30 percent through the 1980s.

THE PROBLEM

Prior to the early 1970s electric utilities were a
"decreasing cost" industry. Because of economies of scale,
electricity produced by new and larger generating plants was
less costly than that produced by older plants. The utilities,
therefore, aggressively promoted sales by offering discount
rates to large volume customers. In some cases, they offered
"kick-backs" to contractors for building "Gold Medallion"
all-electric homes. Since prices remained stable, consumers
generally remained unconcerned about these expansionary practices and the industry doubled in size every ten years.

During the mid-1970s, however, inflation, rising fuel
costs and dramatic increases in the cost of building new
generating plants made electric utilities an "increasing cost"
industry. Nuclear plant construction costs were particularly
inflationary. Each unit of electricity produced by a new generating plant now costs more than electricity from an older plant.
It is now cheaper to save a kilowatt of electricity than to
generate a new one.

Despite the new economic realities, utilities have continued
to push big construction programs, saddling not only themselves,
but consumers with enormous financial burdens.

The electric utility industry is the most capital-intensive
in the economy. On an annual basis, the investor-owned utilities
generally oversee about 20 percent of all new industrial construction, utilize 33 percent of all corporate financing, and
issue about 50 percent of all industrial common stock. While
the utilities need more and more capital, consumers meanwhile
have responded to higher prices by cutting consumption. This
situation has led to what noted energy analyst Amory Lovins
describes as a "spiral of impossibility." Higher rates to
finance new power plants drive down the demand for electricity
the new plants are built to meet.

To escape this "spiral of impossibility," utility activists have proposed reforms ranging from survival tactics --
preventing utilities from shutting off service during winter
months -- to strategies that challenge the need for, and propose substitutes to, big new generating plants.

Promotional rate structures designed to increase sales
by providing discount prices to large users have been a big
target of organized consumers. More than a dozen states have
adopted a reform called "Lifeline Service," which alleviates
some of the unfairness in promotional rates by fixing a low
monthly cost for a set amount of electricity needed by a
typical family.

In the area of ratepayer rights, New York citizens won important protections when the legislature adopted a comprehensive Utility Consumers Bill of Rights in 1981. In addition to restricting winter shut-offs, this legislation also limits utilities from demanding security deposits and requires special procedures before service to senior citizens can be terminated.

Many utilities now petition their state utility commissions for rate increases every year. Frequently the utilities ask permission to charge customers for plants under construction. Most state utility commissions either prohibit or narrowly define this practice; Oregon, Missouri, New Hampshire and most recently, Pennsylvania have passed legislation making "construction work in progress" (CWIP) illegal.

Consumers are often at a disadvantage in challenging the need for new power plants because only the utilities can finance studies of "projected demand." Typically these forecasts overstate demand growth. However, California and 19 other states now require their utility commission or another state agency to conduct formal public hearings and establish an independent electricity forecast.

Utility reformers usually turn to the legislature when state utility commissions prove unresponsive. One major change that activists bring to legislatures is changing the way in which commissioners are selected. Eleven states presently have elected rather than appointed commissions.

The National Energy Act of 1978, mandates utility commission review of load management techniques and automatic fuel adjustment clauses; requires utilities to pay a fair price for electricity they purchase from small power producers; and requires each state to set up a Residential Conservation Service (RCS) offering consumers free or inexpensive home energy audits.

The reforms required by the National Energy Act and others proposed by utility activists, could put brakes on the "spiral of impossibility" and help save the utilities from themselves. But the utilities continue to believe that the short term solution for their "increasing cost" industry is friendly regulators and frequent rate increases. Over the long term the industry hopes that a healthier economy together with discount rates and an aggressive new promotional campaign will reverse the conservation trend of the past ten years and justify their construction programs.

WHAT STATES CAN DO

To Protect Consumer Rights:

° States should establish a Rate Payer Bill of Rights, as in New York, with specific protections involving winter shutoffs, security deposits and termination procedures.

° States should pass legislation to create a Citizens Utility Board (CUB), as did Wisconsin, to represent consumers before the state public utility commission.

° States should require utilities to pay the costs of consumer organizations and their expert witnesses who are granted intervenor status in a utility commission proceeding.

° States should require election of public utility commissioners.

To Reform Rates and Protect Against Unfair Rate Increases:

° States should eliminate promotional rate structures and re-place them with "flat" rates which require everyone to pay the same price per kilowatt hour; or "inverted rates" which increase as the amount used increases. In addition, states should establish a "Lifeline rate" to guarantee a low, fixed monthly bill for small users of electricity.

° States should prohibit automatic fuel adjustment charges.

° States should require utility stockholders to bear the cost of any advertising that does not directly promote energy conservation.

° States should prohibit utilities from charging consumers for taxes utilities do not pay. Federal tax credits have practi-cally eliminated tax liability for many utilities, yet they are allowed to charge consumers for taxes they didn't have to pay.

° States should bar utilities from charging for Construction Work in Progress (CWIP).

To Promote Energy Efficiency and Renewable Resources:

° States should conduct annual public hearings to establish independent forecasts of demand for electricity.

° States should establish a Residential Conservation Service (RCS) program with energy conservation audits performed by citizen organizations or other independent contractors.

° States should provide tax credits and other incentives for conservation and renewable energy investments.

FOR FURTHER INFORMATION

Publications

Model Public Utility Act, Lee Webb. Available for $2.50 from the Conference on Alternative State and Local Policies.

New Initiatives in Energy Legislation: A State by State Guide, 1981-1982. Available from the Conference on Alternative State and Local Policies, $5.95.

Power & Light: Political Strategies for the Solar Transition, David Talbot and Richard E. Morgan, 1981. Available from the Environmental Action Foundation, $6.95.

The Power Line, published monthly by the Environmental Action Foundation. Regular subscription $25.

The Rate Watcher's Guide: How to Shape Up Your Local Utility's Rate Structure, Richard E. Morgan, 1980. Available from the Environmental Action Foundation, $4.95.

Taking Charge: A New Look at Public Power, Richard E. Morgan, Tom Riesenberg and Michael Troutman, 1976. Available from the Environmental Action Foundation, $4.95.

Organizations

CONFERENCE ON ALTERNATIVE STATE AND LOCAL POLICIES, 2000 Florida Ave., N.W., Washington, D.C., 20009 (202) 387-6030, Lee Webb, Director. Publishes studies on energy policy and periodic updates on new state legislation.

ENVIRONMENTAL ACTION FOUNDATION, 724 Dupont Circle Building, Washington, D.C., 20036 (202) 659-1130. The Foundation's Energy Project publishes books, studies and information packets designed for citizens working to reform their local utility.

NATIONAL ASSOCIATION OF STATE UTILITY CONSUMER ADVOCATES, 1424 16th Street, N.W. Suite 105, Washington, D.C. 20036 (202) 462-8800. Maintains information on how officially sanctioned state consumer advocate offices are set up and what they are doing.

NATIONAL CONSUMER LAW CENTER, 11 Beacon Street, Boston, MA 02108 (617) 523-8010. National back-up center for legal service attorneys. The center is especially knowledgeable about energy issues as they affect low-income people.

Prepared by Jeff Brummer.

Labor and Work

Labor Legislation

BACKGROUND FACTS

In May 1983, 10.1 percent of Americans were out of work, according to the Bureau of Labor Statistics.

Among blacks and Hispanics, however, the rate was even higher -- 20.6 percent and 13.8 percent, respectively.

One out of every five Americans will experience unemployment in some form in this year. Unemployment compensation checks will cover only some of the unemployment and only part of the wages lost through unemployment.

Having a job in America doesn't necessarily mean you aren't poor. Eighty percent of the heads of poor households work, but only one-third of them full-time and year round. For poor people who can work, the problem is not just being able to find a job, but being able to find a stable job or a well-paying one.

As a national average, 20.8 percent of non-agriculture related workers belong to a union. New York has the largest percentage of its labor force belonging to a union (39.2 percent); North Carolina the lowest (6.5 percent). A major reason for this low number is the "right-to-work" laws in twenty states which present a major obstacle to union organizing.

Working conditions are often poor and workers are injured or get sick as a result. Many jobs expose workers to the risk of crippling or fatal accidents or potentially fatal diseases. Conservative government estimates suggest that between 115,000 and 200,000 Americans die each year from an occupationally-related accident or disease.

Many workers also face serious employment-related problems because they have relatively little control over their working conditions. Problems can sometimes flow from this common source. The less influence workers have over the pace and organization of work, the more vulnerable they may be to health and safety problems. The less protection workers have against arbitrary dismissal and supervisory abuse, the more difficulties they may have with sudden layoffs and intermittent employment.

THE PROBLEM

Unemployment, low wages, occupational injuries and diseases, and powerful and arbitrary employers are too often the facts of life for America's workers.

Over the last 50 years, the labor movement and liberal organizations have passed precedent-setting national legislation to assist workers in all facets of their life, including the National Labor Relations Act, the DavisBacon Act, Occupational Safety and Health Act, unemployment compensation, worker's compensation, and minimum wage laws. These federal laws certainly need to be broadened and strengthened.

However, at this time an administration is in power in Washington which is committed to weakening all of these protections. It is imperative, therefore, that state governments accept increased responsibility for protecting working people.

Unemployment insurance is a worker's first line of defense against the hardships of unemployment. Benefits are due workers who have enough qualifying wages and yearly work experience to meet their state's minimum conditions, who are free from disqualification on the basis of their separation from their last place of employment and who are ready, willing and able to work.

Although based on federal law, unemployment compensation is administered by the states; and states, controlling many of its most critical features, have in some cases modified the program to improve worker conditions. Victims of lockouts are able to collect benefits in 16 states. The definition of "suitable work" includes fringe benefits in the states of Indiana and Michigan. Twelve states have no waiting period before benefits begin. And in California, a shorttime compensation program exists which mitigates the impact of layoffs by allowing employees to retain workers during temporary slowdowns and pay them partial unemployment insurance benefits.

Maximum state unemployment compensation does not replace a worker's total salary and the minimum weekly amounts are often far below the poverty level. In addition, the complex set of requirements often exclude many from receiving benefits at all, while the maximum number of weeks during which a worker can receive benefits is often limited. The unemployment compensation that the average unemployed person "enjoys" is not the equivalent of a paid vacation but a massive slash in his or her standard of living.

Washington and Ohio have extremely progressive worker's compensation programs because they use a state fund rather than private insurance companies to run the program. Through Washington's exclusive state fund, eligible workers receive $1.05 in benefits for every dollar paid in premiums thanks to the program's investment earnings, which more than offset the entire expense of administering the program. Washington's approach contrasts sharply with states in which private insurers pocket $.48 of every premium dollar, leaving ill and injured workers only $.52 per dollar.

Many workers have little control over the pace and organization of work, health and safety conditions, wage determination and job security. Likewise, employees who wish to "blow the whistle" on illegal consumer or environmental activity by their employer have few powers to resist employer attempts at intimidation, discrimination or retribution for disclosing information. Unionization and collective bargaining, and applying the concept of an employee "bill of rights" to the workplace are two ways to address these problems and increase the "say" that workers have at their jobs.

In the last few years, state legislatures passed a number of interesting pieces of labor oriented legislation. California, Michigan, Ohio, and Wisconsin prohibited the awarding of state contracts to persons or firms found to be in violation of the National Labor Relations Act. Connecticut, Illinois, Louisiana, Ohio, and Oregon now protect workers who report a violation of law or participates in an enforcement proceeding. Maryland passed an important new law protecting farmworkers. Seventeen states strengthened laws against employment discrimination in 1982. Eight states enacted legislation regulating private employment agencies.

Progressives, concerned about the weakening of OSHA and the Reagan-inspired attack on worker health and safety, are also seeking to pass tough right-to-know laws, which would allow employees to know about the hazardous chemicals with which they work. Excellent legislation has already been passed in the cities of Philadelphia and Cincinnati and in the states of California, Connecticut, Maine, Michigan, New York and West Virginia.

WHAT STATES CAN DO

Reforming Unemployment Insurance

° States should increase benefit levels to a higher percent of the claimant's average weekly wage.

° States should increase the number of weeks of compensation coverage. Most states have pegged this level at 26 weeks.

° States should lift "waiting week restrictions" to allow claimants to receive their benefits immediately and eliminate specific "actively seeking work" availability requirements and instead require job search efforts that are appropriate.

° States should enact laws which allow victims of employer lockouts to collect benefits and allow unemployment benefits to be paid to strikers after a seven week waiting period.

° States should protect the jobless' right to obtain benefits. Employers should be required to post notices of unemployment insurance rights in prominent places and hearings should be held prior to a cut-off of benefits.

Protecting and Expanding Workers' Rights

° States with "right-to-work" laws should repeal them.

° States should prohibit the awarding of state contracts to persons or firms found to be in violation of the National Labor Relations Act.

° States should pass a "whistleblowers" protection act which prohibits reprisals against a public or private sector employee who reports any violation of state, local or federal law, or who participates in an investigation, hearing, inquiry or court action.

Establishing Decent Wages

° States should enact or continue "little Davis-Bacon" acts which set prevailing wage standards for construction work financed by state monies.

° States should pass laws to provide for tougher enforcement of state minimum wages.

Increasing Worker Health and Safety

° States should reform their worker's compensation system to include broader eligibility, improved benefits and greater availability of medical care to meet with the standards suggested by the National Commission on State Worker's Compensation Laws.

FOR FURTHER INFORMATION

Publications

AFL-CIO Federationist, AFL-CIO. A monthly magazine which publishes excellent articles on unemployment compensation, worker's compensation, and other labor issues.

The New Right: A Growing Force in State Politics, Will Hunter, 1980. Washington, D.C., Conference on Alternative State and Local Policies. Comprehensive report on "New Right" activities including right-to-work efforts and attacks on prevailing wage.

Putting America Back to Work: What States and Cities Can Do, William Schweke and Lee Webb, 1982. Washington, D.C., Conference on Alternative State and Local Policies, $6.95.

Short Time Compensation and Work Sharing: A New Alternative to Layoffs, 1980, Fred Best and James Mattessich. Washington D.C. Council of State Planning Agencies.

State Workers' Compensation Laws, 1981, US Department of Labor, Employment Standards Division. Reviews state laws.

The Working Poor, David Gordon, 1980, Washington, D.C. Council of State Planning Agencies. Shows what can be done by a state to expand the economy's share of "good jobs."

Organizations

AFL-CIO, 815 16th Street, N.W., Washington, D.C. 20006 (202) 637-5000. Membership organization of private and public sector trade unions, researching national, state, and local labor legislation programs.

CONFERENCE ON ALTERNATIVE STATE AND LOCAL POLICIES, 2000 Florida Avenue, N.W., Washington, D.C. 20009 (202) 387-6030. Lee Webb, Executive Director. Publishes studies on employment and labor programs and periodic updates on new state legislation.

CITIZEN ACTION, 1501 Euclid Avenue, Suite 500, Cleveland, OH 44115 (216) 861-5200. Umbrella organization of nine statewide citizen action groups. Working on range of employment-related issues, including right-to-know legislation and worker's compensation.

Prepared by William Schweke.

Public Employees

Thirteen million people work for state and local government. Until recently, state and local government was the fastest growing sector of our economy, accounting for 16 percent of the U.S. workforce.

Roughly half of all state and local government employees are represented by unions or associations. However, many public workers do not have true collective bargaining rights. The basic protections gained by private sector workers under the National Labor Relations Act 48 years ago are still denied to many public employees.

The number of public employees has been steadily decreasing since 1980, yet few jurisdictions have addressed job security issues such as retraining, recall rights, severance pay and voluntary early retirement.

The growth of technology is also changing working conditions for thousands of public employees. For example, the use of video display terminals speeds up work and creates new health hazards; mechanized refuse collection sometimes results in smaller crews and reduced service; and computerized information services threatens to downgrade the pay and training requirements for librarians.

Although public employees are specifically excluded from Occupational Safety and Health Act protection (that covers all private sector workers), they are included in exposure to a wide variety of hazards. In fact, National Safety Council statistics show that government workers are generally injured over two-and-one-half times as often as private industry workers and those injuries are over twice as severe.

Women, while increasingly present within the civilian workforce, have been segregated into a small number of occupations. Since jobs in which women predominate have been undervalued, there is a substantial gap in earnings between male and female workers. The average woman now earns 59¢ for every $1.00 the average man earns. This disparity has been documented in many public jurisdictions.

As public jurisdictions face reduced revenues from the recession and federal budget cuts, there is an increased effort to contract out public services to private profit-making firms. Contracting out is seen as the answer to high costs and inefficiency, yet often is an excuse for justifying poor management.

THE PROBLEM

Public employees confront three major issues in their work: elimination of jobs; workplace safety and health; and contracting out of work. The denial of the right to collective bargaining often leaves public employees and their representatives powerless to affect these issues.

Some public workers have attained union recognition and the right to collective bargaining in a variety of ways on a state-by-state, city-by-city basis. There are roughly 80,000 local governments in the U.S., 40,000 multi-purpose and 40,000 single-purpose -- aside from the 50 states. Each of these independent jurisdictions has its own wage system, classification plan and benefit levels.

In some jurisdictions bargaining rights were achieved through law -- the first such public sector bargaining law was enacted 23 years ago for local government employees in Wisconsin. In other jurisdictions, bargaining has come about through executive order. And in many states, bargaining rights were achieved on a de facto basis with local governments throughout the state.

This "crazy quilt" system of public sector labor relations is grossly unfair to state and local government employees. Most bargaining laws have at least some inequitable features not contained in private sector bargaining laws. No two state laws are the same; in fact, many states have more than one law covering public workers.

The 1976 U.S. Supreme Court decision in National League of Cities v. Usery chilled the prospects for enactment of federal legislation to establish a rational framework for labor relations in state and local governments. Since this decision, only three states have enacted new collective bargaining legislation for uncovered employees.

The most common argument for denying public employees bargaining rights and the right to strike is that public employees have an adequate alternative to the bargaining process in the various civil service statutes and other ordinances that protect their rights. Yet most aspects of civil service systems are actually the personnel arm of the government -- akin to personnel departments in private enterprises.

Public employees have been decreasing in numbers since 1980. Some of the loss in public employment results from shifts in service delivery from the public to the private sector. Still greater portions of the job loss stem from the federal government's cutbacks in assistance to state and local governments and from the effects of recession and inflation.

The decline in public sector employment threatens the mission of government: to assist and protect the disadvantaged and to provide those goods and services which the private sector is unable or unwilling to supply. For example, workers in institutional and community mental health facilities throughout the country are faced with threats of closures, phase-downs, budget cuts and contracting out. Thousands of workers have been laid off.

Although new technology has the potential to offer safer working conditions, the opportunity to perform more skilled work and more efficient delivery of services, this potential often is often not realized. Experience shows that new technology may make jobs more routine, more unskilled, more unhealthy, lower-paying and more dead-end.

Public employees are not automatically covered by the federal Occupational Safety and Health Act (OSHA) and less than half of the states provide safety and health protections for public employees. When a state does have some coverage, it is often less stringent than that of OSHA. Even where OSHA coverage is available, there is less protection because the Reagan administration is seeking to weaken its provisions.

The historic segregation of women workers in a small number of traditionally female occupations has resulted in substantial disparities between male and female wages. This is certainly true in public employment. This earnings gap is rooted in discrimination, since society systematically undervalues work performed by women. "Women's jobs" pay less than "men's jobs" involving comparable skill, effort and responsibility. Pay equity for all workers cannot be achieved as long as employers deny equitable pay to workers in female-dominated job classifications.

The drive to contract out public services to private, profit-making firms continues at an increasing pace in many jurisdictions throughout the country. With state and local governments facing reduced revenues from the recession and federal budget cuts, many public officials mistakenly view contracting out as the cure-all. While government managers can sometimes achieve short-term solutions which slash personnel costs, they do not consider long-term budgetary and service considerations. In addition, public officials too often exaggerate the value of contracting out as the answer to high costs and inefficiency.

The private delivery of public services has, in many cases, resulted in higher costs, poorer services, decreased accountability and corruption.

WHAT STATES CAN DO

Collective Bargaining

° States should give public sector workers full rights and
protections to organize and bargain collectively in individual states and jurisdictions within the states.

Jobs

° States should negotiate improved job protections and provide
alternatives to layoffs, such as: the rearrangment of budget
priorities and alternative revenue sources; retraining;
transfer rights; severance pay; moving expenses; the use of
attrition instead of layoffs; and voluntary early retirement.

° State should establish career development programs which
provide equitable opportunities for public workers to
obtain promotions.

° States should use trial periods and advance notification
to allow time for careful implementation when new technology
is introduced.

° States should support the use of technologies designed to
improve and expand public services.

Safety and Health at Work

° States should enact laws establishing safety and health plans
covering public employees that incorporate, at a minimum,
federal OSHA standards. States should establish their own
OSHA plans, using Connecticut as an example.

° States should ensure that public employees are provided a
safe and healthy place of work free from recognized or
suspected hazards. The right of employees to refuse unsafe
work should be recognized.

Pay Equity

° States should commit themselves to pay equity and, working
through contract negotiations and administrative actions,
upgrade undervalued job classifications. All job evaluation
studies should investigate the pay equity issue.

Contracting Out

° States should consider the real costs and disadvantages of
proposals to contract out any public work traditionally
performed by public employees, including possible higher
costs, reduced or poorer service, lack of public control
and possible corruption.

FOR FURTHER INFORMATION

Publications

Government for $ale, John Hanrahan. American Federation
of State, County and Municipal Employees, 1977. Details
problems of contracting out government work to the private
sector, especially problems of possible corruption and abuse.

Health and Safety in the Workplace: An AFSCME Handbook,
Research Department, American Federation of State, County and
Municipal Employees, 1983.

Labor-Management Relations in State and Local Governments,
Bureau of the Census, Special Studies No. 102, November 1981.
Analyzes state and local government agreements: the number of
agreements between government and unions and the kinds of
governments concerned.

Manual on Pay Equity: Raising Wages for Women's Work.
Conference on Alternative State and Local Policies, 1980, $8.95.
Comprehensive manual of facts and figures, detailed analysis of
federal, state and local laws and strategies for organizing.

Pay Equity: A Union Issue for the 1980s. American
Federation of State, County and Municipal Employees, 1980.

Summary of Public Sector Labor Relations Policies, U.S.
Department of Labor, Labor-Management Services Administration,
1981. Reviews status of laws in each state with respect to
bargaining rights, strike policy, etc.

Organizations

AMERICAN FEDERATION OF STATE, COUNTY AND MUNICIPAL EMPLOYEES,
1625 L Street, N.W., Washington, D.C., 20036 (202) 452-4800.
Linda Lampkin, Director, Department of Research. Excellent
source of information on policies affecting public employees.
Does lobbying and provides political support.

NATIONAL EDUCATION ASSOCIATION, 1201 16th Street, N.W.,
Washington, D.C., 20036 (202) 822-7300. Largest organization
of teachers. Provides information on wages, salaries and
issues affecting public education.

PUBLIC EMPLOYEE DEPARTMENT, AFL-CIO, 815 16th Street, N.W.,
Washington, D.C., 20006 (202) 393-2820. Provides updates on
issues affecting public employees.

Prepared by Linda Lampkin.

Workplace Safety and Health

<u>BACKGROUND FACTS</u>

Death and disease in the workplace is an omnipresent fact of life for millions of American workers. Scientific research conducted in the 1970s leads to one conclusion: the magnitude of the occupational injury and disease problem is greater than the framers of the Occupational Safety and Health Act in the 1960s ever expected.

Problems such as excessive exposure to lead, cotton dust, mercury and silica have not disappeared and new issues keep surfacing -- for example, discovery of brain tumors in petrochemical industry workers.

Reasonable estimates of job-related cancer suggest that as many as 40,000-50,000 workers will die in 1983. All these cancers could have been prevented if exposure to workplace carcinogens had not occurred. Moreover, the human toll may grow worse in the decades ahead. Because the average latency for human cancer is twenty years or more, it is likely that current cancer deaths are a reflection of past exposures during early expansion of the petrochemical industry. Attention has also focused on reproductive impairment or damage to workers' children from parental exposures. Thus, the precautions taken in the next few years will determine whether occupational cancer will rise in the 21st century.

Cancer, reproductive impairment, chronic lung disease and neurologic toxicity all have emerged as major occupational health problems. In addition, concern has grown about new health hazards, such as indoor air pollution, job-related stress, health effects of new energy technology, radiation (both ionizing and non-ionizing), hazards of machine-paced work and continuous work on visual display terminals.

The passage of the Occupational Safety and Health Act (OSHA) of 1970 was heralded as landmark legislation which assured for every worker the right to a safe and healthful workplace. One often-stated argument for the enactment of federal legislation was the dismal performance of state occupational safety and health programs in protecting the lives of workers. As a result, the federal government was given a major role in the new legislation; states were allowed to run their own programs only if they were proven to be "at least as effective" as the federal OSHA efforts.

THE PROBLEM

Occupational health gains were made during the years of the Carter administration with new programs and regulations put in place or proposed. Under Reagan however, OSHA is undergoing planned disassembly and decline. Enforcement, training and education, standard setting, protection of worker rights to participate, funding, staffing and research have all been cut. For example, the number of inspectors has declined by 29 percent; monthly inspections by 17 percent; follow-up inspections by 68 percent and serious citations by 27 percent. Some regulations have been withdrawn; others are not being enforced.

As a result, we look at some state and local remedies for occupational health problems. With the Reagan administration's focus on deregulation rather than protecting workers' health, the need to improve state programs once again has become paramount. States ironically need to play an increasingly important role in protecting the gains of the 1970s and in expanding worker protection.

In general, state record keeping systems are not designed to facilitate recognition of work-related problems. Improved data collection systems are mandatory if effective research is to be carried out to identify and assess work-related disease. In 1976, California started requiring employers to register certain carcinogens they used in the workplace. California has recently passed legislation which establishes a Birth Defects Registry designed to quantify increased risk to reproduction from toxic substance exposure. Connecticut operates a Tumor Registry and Los Angeles County has a tumor registry with promising experience in identifying high risk populations.

The acid test for workers' rights is whether workers have the right to know the identity and the hazards of substances with which they work. Most of these laws have basically the same purpose: to ensure that workers know the hazards of substances they work with and that the government and local citizens know where toxic materials are used or handled.

State and local toxics laws are most useful if they are enacted to protect both workers and the public. State and local laws with a broad scope that includes protecting the public health and adequately preparing for local emergency services can protect these laws from federal preemption.

Workers can be reluctant to participate in medical surveillance programs if they fear they might lose their jobs if they turn out to be ill. Right-to-know legislation provides for access to information but does not require a

duty to warn. "Duty to warn" legislation would represent a
significant improvement over the current important but limited
right-to-know statutes. Employers should have a clear duty
to inform workers when they are exposed to hazardous substances
or conditions rather than simply make information available.
To be most effective, such legislation should include both
civil and criminal penalties

   States should consider additional remedial legislation
to expand worker rights beyond those guaranteed by OSHA,
including:

° Increasing the maximum penalties for willful failure to
  abate repeated and serious violations of the OSH Act.

° Expanding workers' right-to-refuse hazardous work. Workers
  who face life-threatening hazards including exposure to
  carcinogens (the effect of which may not be manifested
  until ten to twenty years later) should have the right-of-
  refusal to work where an imminent hazard exists. When they
  refuse to work because of an imminent danger, their pay
  should not be docked.

° Adding provisions on rate retention and "walk around" pay.
  Rate retention (including no loss of wages or benefits if
  temporarily removed from the job because of an occupational
  illness) encourages workers to participate in the company's
  medical surveillance program because workers do not fear
  being penalized if an occupational illness is discovered.
  They can be temporarily removed from their jobs until tests
  show their health has improved. This unique provision is a
  part of OSHA's lead standard.

  Walk around pay is based on similar considerations. Legislation which guarantees an employee representative pay
  during an inspection by an OSHA compliance officer will
  augment the right to participate in an OSHA walk around.

° Safety and health legislation designed to increase workers'
  rights and participation would expand the private right of
  action of workers facing unsafe or unhealthful work conditions.
  Enabling legislation will be required in most states to
  ensure citizens' rights of redress.

° Revenue for state safety and health programs could be generated through worker's compensation programs in which insurance premiums from industry designed to fund various programs
  would be based upon the size of a particular payroll and the
  actuarial status of the company. The state of Washington is
  a prime example of the use of funds from worker's compensation
  to support research and education programs.

WHAT STATES CAN DO

State OSHA Programs

° States with OSHA programs should consider increasing maximum penalties for willful failure to abate and repeated citations.

° States should adopt legislation guaranteeing walk-around pay and rate retention during temporary medical removal from jobs.

Right to Know Legislation

° States should pass worker right-to-know legislation to ensure that 1) workers know the identity and the hazards of the substances with which they work, and 2) that the public is informed of toxic chemicals being used.

° States should pass legislation which supplements right-to-know legislation with an affirmative duty to warn and gives workers the right to refuse to perform unsafe work.

State Centers

° States should establish Centers for Occupational Safety and Health Research, Service and Training. California has adopted legislation which established two state-funded occupational health centers to upgrade and expand the resources of the state.

Legal Rights

° States should enact legislation which provides for private right of action by workers in order that they sue to correct hazards rather than being wholly dependent on departments of labor or health.

Record Keeping

° States should adopt legislation to establish birth defects, spontaneous abortion and cancer registries which are coded for industry and occupation. In addition, they should ensure that death certificates are coded for industry and occupation to facilitate identification of work-related mortality.

Reproductive Rights

° States should enact legislation creating or strengthening laws applicable to the use of carcinogens and to chemicals which cause reproductive impairment.

FOR FURTHER INFORMATION

Publications

Ashford, Nicholas, <u>Crisis in the Workplace: Occupational Disease and Injury</u>, MIT Press: Cambridge, Mass., 1976. Describes the role of state programs prior to enactment of OSHA; and generally is a useful source book on occupational safety and health.

Davis, D. et al., in <u>Banbury Report 9 - Quantification of Occupational Cancer</u>, edited by Richard Peto and Marvin Schneiderman, Cold Spring Harbor Laboratory, 1981. A thorough discussion of the problems in estimating cancer causes. The entire report is a useful source book on occupational cancer.

Kaminski, R. et al., <u>American Journal of Public Health</u>, 71, 525-526, 1981. Discussion of coding death certificates.

<u>Labor Studies Journal</u>, 6(1), Spring 1981. Edited by Steven Deutsch. The entire journal is devoted to the theme of occupational safety and health. The final three articles are devoted to resources. Available from Transaction Periodicals Consortium, Box L, Rutgers University, New Brunswick, NJ, 08903.

<u>Reproductive Hazards in the Workplace - A Resource Guide</u>, Coalition for The Reproductive Rights of Workers, 1971 I Street, N.W., Washington, D.C., 20006. A resource guide to issues of reproductive impairment from chemical and physical agents in the workplace.

Organizations

AFL-CIO DEPARTMENT OF OCCUPATIONAL SAFETY AND HEALTH, Room 507, 815 16th Street, N.W., Washington, D.C., 20006 (202) 637-5174. Contact: Peg Seminario. Extensive material on right-to-know laws and the Reagan administration's policies on occupational safety and health.

HAZARD EVALUATION SYSTEM AND INFORMATION SERVICE (THESIS), 2151 Berkeley Way, Room 504, Berkeley, CA, 94704 (415) 540-2012. Cancer and reproductive impairment information, including information on the California Birth Defects Registry and California Cancer Control legislation.

Prepared by John Froines.

Education

Public Education

America's system of public education is facing a critical period.

Maintaining and expanding our public school system in the midst of massive cuts in federal assistance, a deep economic recession and strong citizen opposition to higher state and local taxes is a difficult task.

The states' role in financing education is growing more important. In the 1982-83 school year for example, states contributed half of all public school revenues, local sources roughly 42 percent and the federal government a little less than eight percent.

States and local school districts face difficult problems picking up the burden of federal cuts and maintaining funding for their existing programs. State surpluses fell from $11 billion in 1980 to $4.7 billion in 1981, then slid to a minimal $1.9 billion by the end of 1982. Only 15 states have surpluses, with the bulk of the money concentrated in oil-producing Texas and Alaska. Twenty-two states have deficits totaling more than $5.7 billion and only 13 states expect to break even this fiscal year. The majority of the states are attempting to face this crisis situation by scaling back budgets, implementing hiring freezes or laying off state workers.

In addition to the problems brought on by the recession, state and local governments are under pressure to pick up the costs of many non-education programs cut from the federal budget. For example, staggering new demands to rehabilitate state and local infrastructure will increasingly compete with education and other human services programs.

Cutbacks in federal education programs will hurt the quality of education in schools across the country. While local districts receive on the average only about eight percent of their funds from federal programs, those programs are critical because they concentrate on assistance to the disadvantaged, the disabled and the needy.

States vary widely in the amount and kind of education they provide. The amount of financial assistance, the requirements established for students and teachers and the standards of quality can be as different as night and day. On the average in 1980, states spent roughly $390 per capita on education. But in that year, Alaska spent $1,497, while New Hampshire spent only $202.

THE PROBLEM

The founders of this nation were indeed wise when they
made the education of the nation's citizens a national imperative. They saw it as a most effective tool in the development
of basic skills required in the building of a nation, and the
means to meet the need for a skilled and educated workforce.

Our classrooms, school libraries and laboratories are,
after all, critical institutions. At their best, they not
only train the minds of our children and hone their skills but
they are also powerful institutions advancing our health, our
safety, our economic well-being, our common defense, our rights
and our freedoms. They enrich the nation's culture. They
inculcate the ideals and the value systems of our democracy.
They inspire commonality of purpose.

The federal role in education has increased over the years
to meet national priorities. This has meant passage of such
important legislation as the National Defense Education Act in
1958 and the GI "Bill of Rights" following World War II. Even
with these comprehensive programs, however, federal aid has
never averaged more than eight percent of all education
expenditures in the country.

But the Reagan administration has made this vital aid a
target. In his FY 83 budget proposal, the President attempted
to cut 33 percent from federal education programs. Congressional intervention spared a number of the cuts, although
massive decreases were made in many programs. But Congressional response and an accompanying public outcry tempered
the President's actions in his FY 84 budget proposal.

But, President Reagan is now calling for implementation
of a federal tuition tax credits program, which would be a
boondoggle for the nation's wealthy and upper middle-classes,
and for its private schools. By conservative estimates, it
would cost the nation's taxpayers some $1.3 billion when
fully implemented and would mean that the federal government,
on a per pupil basis, would provide more assistance to private
school students than it now does to public school students.

Similarly, voucher plans, proposed on and off for several
decades now, would extend the public funding of schools to
include parochial and private schools by allowing parents of
elementary and secondary school children to use their voucher
-- worth a designated amount -- in a private, parochial or
public school.

A great deal of public debate has centered in the past
year on educational deficiencies, especially in the areas
of math, science and technological skill readiness. During
this period, even conservatives have been expressing misgivings

about a diminished investment in education. Denis P. Doyle of the American Enterprise Institute, for instance, described the cutbacks in higher education spending as unwise public policy when no workable alternative is proposed by the Reagan administration. Failure to invest in the education of doctors, physicists, mathematicians and engineers, he says, will mean those skills will not be there to meet our future needs. "It takes 20 years to train the next generation of engineers, scientists and linguists," he notes.

One of the main goals in federal education programs has been to ensure equity of access to education for all the nation's citizens. But those federal programs are now being systematically dismantled or cut back. Translated into human terms, these losses in funding mean literally hundreds of thousands of young people denied the opportunity to better prepare themselves for the future.

Public concern and Congressional leadership has also been key to bringing to the fore the need for a federal commitment to reemphasize education in math and science, communications and technology to better prepare our nation's citizens for increasing international economic competition brought about largely through the revolution in technology. This has led to a number of federal legislative proposals aimed at assisting schools at a time when a diminishing federal role seems more the call of the day.

However, the current economic recession, cutbacks in federally-supported social programs, including education and federal tax cuts, have hit states hard. These measures have had a profound effect on the financial capabilities of states and cities to maintain, let alone expand, existing commitments to social programs without huge tax increases.

This greater financial responsibility of the states will mean that state political leaders will be facing harder choices. Allocations for vital functions such as bridge and road repair will come into direct competition with funding for social and human service programs such as welfare, food stamps and education. While it is clear that infrastructure needs must be met, legislators cannot lose sight of the fact that education is also an investment in the future of the state and indeed of the country.

Despite these difficult choices, state legislators must keep quality education for all students throughout their state as a top priority. States and local school districts facing bleak financial futures may tend to turn back the clock on progressive moves aimed at equalizing per pupil expenditures and closing the disparities between wealthy and poor school districts. States should aim for a high quality education for all students regardless of the wealth of their particular school district.

WHAT STATES CAN DO

Maintain Adequate Funding and Equity

° States should maintain and expand programs that attempt to
equalize the funding availability for all districts so that
students in poorer areas will have the same access to
quality education as students in wealthier districts.

° States should maintain and expand programs that provide
equity of access and, when necessary, remedial assistance
to minority and disadvantaged students.

° States should maintain and expand education and rehabilitation programs for the handicapped.

° States should maintain and expand vocational and adult
education programs.

Collective Bargaining

° States should enact legislation guaranteeing the right of
collective bargaining to teachers and other employees
in the state's public school systems.

Teacher Education

° States should continue and expand adequate funding for
teacher training and education programs at state colleges
and universities.

° States should provide adequate funding for programs of
continuing education for teachers.

Tuition Tax Credits

° States should defeat legislation that would provide tuition
tax credits for students attending private schools.

Voucher Plan

° States should defeat legislation that would create educational
"voucher" plans because they would fatally weaken America's
public school system.

FOR FURTHER INFORMATION

Publications

1981 Annual Report, Advisory Panel on Financing Elementary and Secondary Education, P.O. Box 19125, Washington, D.C., 20036.

The Federal Education Budget, An NEA Policy Paper, National Education Association, Government Relations, 1201 16th Street, N.W., Washington, D.C. 20036, 202-822-7300. This publication analyzes the impact of federal budget priorities and the new federalism on education.

The Federal Role in Education, An NEA Policy Paper, This paper traces the history of the federal role in education, explains the rationale for it and discusses the wisdom of maintaining a Cabinet department.

Rankings of the States, 1982, National Education Association, Research Department, 1201 16th Street, N.W., Washington, D.C. 20036.

Organizations

AMERICAN FEDERATION OF TEACHERS, 11 Dupont Circle, N.W., Washington, D.C. 20036 (202) 797-4400. An excellent source for information on problems affecting public education.

EDUCATION COMMISSION OF THE STATES, 1860 Lincoln St., Denver, CO 80295 (303) 830-3785. E.C.S. works with state political and educational leaders to improve policies in education, and serves as a clearinghouse for policies and proposals on educational reform.

NATIONAL ASSOCIATION OF STATE BOARDS OF EDUCATION, 444 North Capitol Street, Room 256, Washington, D.C. 20001 (202) 624-5845. N.A.S.B.E. provides information to members on governmental activity vis-a-vis education and prints special projects publications on educational problems of the gifted, talented, handicapped and the underprivileged.

NATIONAL EDUCATION ASSOCIATION, 1201 16th Street, N.W., Washington, D.C. 20036 (202) 822-7300. NEA is an excellent source for information on problems affecting public education.

Prepared by Linda Tarr-Whelan and Andrea DiLorenzo.

Students

Twelve million students attend 3,200 colleges, universities, two-year, professional and technical schools. These students and schools are found in virtually every congressional and legislative district in the country. California, Florida, Illinois, Massachusetts, Michigan, Ohio, New York and Texas each have student populations of 400,000 or more.

In addition to postsecondary students, 18 million people -- nearly 12 percent of the adult population -- participate in some form of adult education. As "lifelong learning" becomes more common, more adults will turn to colleges and universities to gain job retraining, new job skills and further intellectual development.

Educational opportunities for economically disadvantaged students grew dramatically in the 1960s and 1970s, made possible by expansion of federal financial assistance programs. By 1980, over four million students received aid from three need-based federal programs -- more than three times the number of recipients in 1976.

The Reagan administration, however, has severely restricted access to higher education by its enormous cuts in financial assistance programs. Funding for federal student aid (excluding Guaranteed Student Loans) dropped 32 percent between FY 80 and FY 83. Programs helping low-income students -- Pell Grants and campus-based aid -- fell 23 percent during that period. These cutbacks would have been even more devastating if Congress had not rejected the original Reagan proposals.

In contrast to their counterparts in the 1960s, students today are often portrayed as apathetic or conservative. While campuses are not the hotbeds of political activity they were 15 years ago, student activism is still alive and strong. Using check-off systems on university registration forms, students have funded stable, professionally-staffed nonprofit organizations to represent their interests and to expand educational opportunities beyond the classroom.

Public Interest Research Groups (PIRGs), which conduct research, lobbying and organizing on consumer issues, can be found on over 120 campuses in 20 states. State Student Associations (SSAs) lobby legislatures for student interests, especially on financial aid questions. Many states, including California, New York and Pennsylvania, boast influential student lobbies.

THE PROBLEM

Several issues are important to large numbers of students although no overriding issues dominate college campuses as civil rights and Vietnam did in the 1960s.

The most important student concern is the question of whether they can afford to attend college. Almost half of all students receive some form of government financial aid. Yet the Reagan administration has reversed the long-standing American commitment to provide a college education to any qualified person, regardless of income.

The American Council on Education (ACE) reports that, in addition to the Reagan administration's previous drastic cuts in financial assistance, the administration now proposes to freeze federal higher education spending and institute policies leading to "further restriction of eduational opportunities." The Reagan FY 84 proposals would, according to an ACE report:

° "Radically alter the way student aid is distributed ... By the Administration's own estimates, the net effect would be to eliminate approximately 1 million student aid awards."

° Eliminate graduate fellowships for minorities and women.

° Cut funding by 77 percent for special services to economically disadvantaged students.

° Double the loan origination fee for graduate students receiving Guaranteed Student Loans.

° Award 400,000 fewer Pell Grants for disadvantaged students than were previously available.

College costs are currently rising 15 to 20 percent. The average cost of attending a public university is almost $4,000 annually, private college costs average $7,000 per year. These escalating costs have forced many colleges to reverse long-held policies of admitting students regardless of financial need. Many states have raised their tuition and room and board fees to meet budgetary problems.

Students, too, have had to change their college plans, based on financial considerations. A Chronicle of Higher Education study of fall 1981 enrollments found that some students who would have preferred private colleges are attending state universities; students who might have gone to state universities are opting for community colleges.

Some students are abandoning graduate education altogether. Financial aid cutbacks and tuition hikes have combined to discourage low-income students from pursuing graduate study. Dr. John Sanderson warned in the New England Journal of Medicine that the medical profession could become "almost entirely the province of the very wealthy" if state and federal student aid is not increased.

Opponents of student financial aid traditionally raise two arguments. First, they argue, in the words of David Stockman, that "if people want to go to college bad enough, then there's opportunity and responsibility on their part to finance their way the best they can." These critics don't explain how millions of students can find adequately-paying jobs when the adult unemployment rate is the worst since 1941.

Financial aid critics, including the conservative Heritage Foundation, also maintain that government has no obligation to aid students, since, in their view, education is more a private than a public benefit. This argument ignores the crucial importance of a well-educated population to a modern, technological society. If the U.S. is to compete effectively in the world economy, it must have skilled, trained citizens. Though Japan has only half our population, it currently graduates 50 percent more students with engineering degrees. The U.S. graduates fewer doctorates in computer science than we did in the mid-1970s.

Students face other barriers in their path to higher education. Lack of campus child care facilities keeps women and disadvantaged students from attending college. Federal programs ensuring equal opportunity to women (Title IX) and disabled students (Section 504) have been neglected or opposed by the Reagan administration.

Participation in university decision-making and control of student fees are also major student concerns. In many states students are denied voting representation on state university boards of trustees. Students have also been denied the right to control their fee systems and to voluntarily tax themselves to fund student-run, nonprofit organizations.

Finally, students face discrimination in their roles as citizens. Some localities prevent students from voting in their college communities; students are, in many cases, exempted from minimum wage protections; and landlords may discriminate against students seeking off-campus housing (such as prohibiting more than three unrelated people from living under the same roof).

State policies should guarantee student's basic rights. With the Reagan administration's abdication of the federal role in higher education, states must also take action to ensure the right of any qualified person to higher education. In the 1980s the decisions of state policy-makers will determine whether America has the well-educated population essential to both the national economy and a democratic society.

WHAT STATES CAN DO

Ensuring Equal Access to Education

° States should set up low-interest loan or grant programs for
  students. Rhode Island is using bonds to fund a new $100
  million loan program. Illinois has launched a loan program
  for private college students.

  States should also investigate the use of public pension
  funds to support loan or grant programs for children of public
  employees.

° States should establish programs to fund campus child care
  services and, where necessary, require schools to provide
  services to help disadvantaged students. These services
  should be available at night for part-time students.
  California's Campus Child Care Development Act supports
  child care at public and private institutions. The state
  has also directed public vocational colleges to give special
  child care services to students to aid them in surmounting
  social and economic obstacles to education.

° States should pass legislation equivalent to the federal
  Title IX program to protect educational opportunities for
  women from federal neglect. Alaska and Nebraska are among
  the states with "mini Title IX" programs.

Protecting Student Rights

° States should legally recognize the right of students to
  control their own fees; the Wisconsin law is the best model.
  States should reject legislation prohibiting the use of
  student fees for nonpartisan political education activities.

° States should require student voting representation on state
  university boards of trustees.

° States should pass legislation ensuring the right of students
  to register and vote in their college communities.

Other

° States should establish programs to expand university job
  retraining opportunities. Such programs can be especially
  valuable in communities hit by plant closings. New Jersey
  has established a program to expand job retraining through
  community colleges.

FOR FURTHER INFORMATION

Publications

Cognition, National Student Educational Fund, three times a year, free. A newsletter examining policy issues affecting students.

The College Student and Higher Education Policy: What Stake and What Purpose, Carnegie Foundation for the Advancement of Teaching, 1975.

Policies for the Future: State Policies, Regulations and Resources Related to the Achievement of Educational Equity for Females and Males. Available from the Resource Center for Sex Equity, Council of Chief State School Officers, 379 Hall of the States, 400 N. Capitol St., N.W., Washington, D.C. 20001.

The Real Subminimum Wage, 1981. Includes material on the student subminimum wage. Available for $2.50 from the National Center for Jobs and Justice, 1638 R St., N.W., Washington, D.C. 20009.

Organizations

AMERICAN COUNCIL ON EDUCATION, 1 Dupont Circle, Washington, D.C. 20036 (202) 833-4700. Comprises most the nation's colleges and universities. A wealth of material on student financial assistance and effects of the Reagan cutbacks. Publishes Higher Education and National Affairs weekly ($30 per year).

AMERICANS FOR DEMOCRATIC ACTION YOUTH CAUCUS, 1411 K St., N.W., Washington, D.C. 20005 (202) 638-6447.

COALITION OF INDEPENDENT COLLEGE AND UNIVERSITY STUDENTS, 1730 Rhode Island Ave., N.W., Washington, D.C. 20036 (202) 659-1747.

NATIONAL COMMISSION ON STUDENT FINANCIAL ASSISTANCE, 412 First St., S.E., Washington, D.C. 20003. Will provide information on state student financial assistance programs.

NATIONAL STUDENT EDUCATIONAL FUND, 2000 P St., N.W., Room 300, Washington, D.C. 20036 (202) 785-1856. Kathy Downey, President. Conducts research and organizing on student issues. Has contacts for State Student Associations.

UNITED STATES STUDENT ASSOCIATION, 2000 P St., N.W., Room 305, Washington, D.C. 20036 (202) 775-8943. Janice Fine, National Chair.

Prepared by David Jones.

Civil and Human Rights

Citizens with Disabilities

BACKGROUND FACTS

An estimated 36 to 45 million persons with disabilities live in the United States. Every community has a significant number of disabled persons with a variety of needs.

Many disabled people are prevented from becoming active participants in their community by the following barriers: architectural design, lack of ability to communicate with others, insecurity of basic survival needs, lack of transportation, exclusion and other forms of discrimination, lack of community-based services and inadequate education.

Research shows that for every dollar spent on rehabilitation and training programs for disabled persons, six dollars are recaptured in tax revenues when the disabled person begins work. Yet current cuts in social programs will reduce the number of disabled people who receive training. Similarly, the future of independent living programs, aimed at enhancing the self-sufficiency of disabled people, is in doubt.

Recent decisions by the Reagan administration pertaining to auto safety, occupational health and safety, and environmental protection will increase the number of disabled persons, either from birth defects, accident or exposure to toxic chemicals. Yet as resources for human services become scarce, disabled people may lose the services and benefits they need to be more independent.

Federal legislation mandates that disabled children receive a free and appropriate public education with services and equipment to meet their needs, but the federal government has not provided adequate funding to insure disabled children of their rights.

For people with severe and multiple handicaps, to provide community-based services in home-like settings is cheaper than to put them in large, isolated institutions. Yet, even though a small percentage of severely disabled people live in large institutions, the bulk of federal money goes to such institutions.

The disabled community has convinced the Reagan administration not to modify Section 504 regulations, the major civil rights provisions on which disabled people rely. However, the Department of Justice has shown a reluctance to enforce these regulations.

THE PROBLEM

As the role of the federal government in relation to the states and local governments is changing, and as budget cuts are endangering the existence of community services, the gains of disabled persons in the U.S. are in jeopardy.

The Reagan administration has accelerated the review process for Supplemental Security Income (SSI) and Supplemental Security for the Disabled Income (SSDI) claimants in an effort to drastically reduce the number of beneficiaries.

Thousands of disabled persons have lost their only source of income without a face-to-face examination by the reviewers. Of those who have appealed their terminations, a vast majority have won because they are not able to work. However, many do not appeal. And even those who win their appeals must wait for months, living on nothing, before their cases are heard.

The 1970s marked the beginning of innovative legislation and programs recognizing that an individual's potential was not predetermined by severity or type of disability.

The appropriate government response in the 1980s to the problems of the disabled is to promote the potential of each person. New approaches include: prohibiting discrimination against qualified disabled persons at the federal and state levels; expanding the coverage of rehabilitation programs to insure severely disabled people are trained for jobs; eliminating disincentives in benefit programs which prevent disabled people from seeking jobs; assuring that federally-funded buildings, including federal housing, are accessible to and usable by disabled people and creation of independent living programs, operated by disabled people at the local level, to provide advocacy and services. Disabled people could live as independently as possible in their own communities, rather than in nursing homes and institutions.

The rationale behind recent policy innovation is that disabled people have a right, as citizens of this country, to expect a minimum level of support and civil rights protection from the government. This approach rejects past notions that disabled people are best served by charities and welfare programs (which do not envision the disabled person as a valuable community member with potential for leadership and self-sufficiency). It also rejects the medical approach to resolving the disability problems, in which disabled people are viewed as sick or deviant and must be cured or taken care of.

Implementation of these civil rights protections and innovative new programs have been opposed with two principal arguments: 1) that the cost of providing services to and making accommodations for disabled people is too high, and 2) that there aren't that many disabled people who want to actively participate in their communities, travel or work.

The cost argument ignores the enormous costs currently being paid for programs that do little or nothing to increase the self-sufficiency and skills of disabled people. These include: state hospitals for people with mental retardation and other disabilities in which, historically, abuses and regression have been the rule; benefit programs like Supplemental Security Income, which keep people dependent on benefits for the rest of their lives, rather than actively seeking training and eventual employment; medical benefit programs which do not pay for independent living training and equipment and which instead force people into expensive hospital settings for medical care; expensive, separate special schools for disabled children to which they must be bused, at additional cost; separate transportation services which require additional drivers, vehicles, fuel and other costs. These and other expensive programs are designed to keep disabled people outside of the mainstream of community life.

It is impossible to ignore the fact that there are millions of disabled people in this country and that there are expenses involved in responding to their existence. State and local policy makers must decide whether that response is planned to increase their ability to participate in the community or to further segregate, isolate and ensure that they will never be able to contribute.

In the coming decades, as the numbers of disabled people increase, this issue will become more crucial. The issue, then, is how money is spent, rather than how much.

The second argument -- that disabled people don't really want to take advantage of opportunities to participate actively -- ignores the growing movement of disabled people who are organizing at the grassroots level. There are dozens of disabled people's organizations in most states and they have changed from the social clubs into politically active and sophisticated groups.

Increasing numbers of disabled people have enrolled at colleges and universities in pursuit of skills and degrees that will yield jobs. As disabled people receive an education, their expectations rise. This leads to growing numbers of disabled persons who can take advantage of increased accessibility and opportunities.

WHAT STATES CAN DO

Civil Rights

° States should pass legislation prohibiting discrimination
  on the basis of disability. States must recognize that
  discrimination against disabled people poses a substantial
  barrier to their independence. Many employers, for instance,
  use old and arbitrary hiring policies which screen out
  qualified disabled job applicants.

Education

° States should pass legislation ensuring the educational
  rights of disabled children. State legislation should
  contain the same rights, procedures and safeguards as the
  federal Education for All Handicapped Children Act. As
  the federal government reduces its role, states must ensure
  that disabled children receive a free and appropriate
  education.

Independent Living

° States should enact legislation creating independent living
  programs. These programs, with relatively small budgets,
  provide crucial services which keep disabled persons out of
  residential or medical facilities costing much more.

° States should restructure their in-home support services to
  allow disabled people to hire, supervise, or fire their own
  attendants, who provide homemaker, chore-type services.
  Such a program has been in effect in California for nearly a
  decade. Because the disabled person is in direct control
  of the attendant, there is no bureaucratic structure to
  take away flexibility to arrange for one's own needs. The
  costs of implementing such a system are less than using
  private companies which often charge high administrative
  fees.

Access to Medical Care

° States should maintain adequate funding for Medicaid because
  people with disabilities rely on federal and state medicaid
  for mobility, medical care and in-house support services.
  Without these support services, people with disabilities
  are in jeopardy of living in nursing homes or other
  restricted environments.

FOR FURTHER INFORMATION

Publications

Handicapping America: Barriers to People, Frank Bowe, Harper and Row, 1978.

"Independent Living: From Social Movement to Analytic Paradigm," Gerben DeJong, Archives of Physical Medicine and Rehabilitation, October 1979.

The Legal Rights of Handicapped Persons, Robert L. Bergdorf, Paul H. Brookes Publishing Co., 1980.

The Unexpected Minority, John Glideman and William Roth, Harcourt Brace Javanovich, 1980.

Organizations

ASSOCIATION FOR RETARDED CITIZENS, 1522 K Street, N.W., Washington, D.C. 20005. An association with chapters in the states; a strong advocate for the rights of persons with mental retardation and services for them. Their governmental affairs office has information about legislation at the state and federal level.

CHILDREN'S DEFENSE FUND, 122 C Street N.W., Washington, D.C. 20001. Legal rights organization with an excellent component specializing in the rights of disabled children, especially in education.

DISABILITY RIGHTS CENTER, 1346 Connecticut Avenue, N.W., Washington, D.C. 20036, Evan Kemp, Director. A legal rights group focusing on consumer rights for medical devices and federal affirmative action laws for disabled workers.

DISABILITY RIGHTS EDUCATION AND DEFENSE FUND, INC., 2032 San Pablo Avenue, Berkeley, CA 94702. Robert Funk, Director/ Attorney. A legal rights and public policy organization focusing on the civil rights of disabled persons.

UNITED CEREBRAL PALSY ASSOCIATIONS, INC., 2021 K Street, N.W., Washington, D.C. 20006. Information and programs about state and local policies that provide for maximum self-sufficiency for persons with severe disabilities.

Prepared by Deborah Kaplan.

Civil Rights

The status of civil rights in America is at a critical point.

In the 1960s and early 1970s this nation's commitment to equality of opportunity and to prevention of discrimination based on race, sex, age, religion, national origin or disability was translated into a series of laws designed to transform the commitment into a reality backed by federal enforcement.

The commitment remained firm in the 1970s. Congress, under the leadership of Presidents Nixon, Ford and Carter, passed further legislation to fill gaps in the basic laws and to strengthen the enforcement powers of the federal government. Those federal agencies charged with enforcing civil rights laws actively pursued abuses and substantial funds were appropriated to help them do their job.

These gains are rapidly being eroded under a tide of conservatism, apathy and a loss of confidence in the American political system.

In all three areas of major civil rights legislation -- voting, housing and employment -- legislative protections are being "evaluated." For months, the existence of the Voting Rights Act of 1965 hung precariously in the balance on Capitol Hill; tougher anti-discriminatory housing legislation has been forestalled; and the backbone of societal equality -- employment discrimination legislation -- is facing attack from both the administration and a seemingly less vigilant Supreme Court.

Equality in the workplace has not become a reality. 66,569 charges of discrimination were filed nationwide in fiscal year 1979-1980, according to the Equal Employment Opportunity Commission.

The unemployment rates of minorities remains at twice the level of whites and women in the labor market earned only 60 percent the income of their male counterparts.

Over two-thirds of our disabled citizens are unemployed or underemployed.

THE PROBLEM

To protect and expand civil rights in America, action in the 1980s is needed. Expanded litigation is certainly one strategy. But perhaps the best is new legislation and stronger enforcement of existing legislation. The bite must be put back into existing civil rights legislation. Watchdog groups must be established to ensure that civil rights legislation and its enforcement are constant protections.

In times of economic recession, those groups historically out of the mainstream of economic and social equality are affected to a greater degree than more affluent groups. Thus unemployment rates for blacks, Hispanics and Mexican Americans, which have always been higher than those for white Americans, continue to increase. Although women have achieved some progress in the workplace, the defeat of ERA indicates, for the near future at least, that women will still trail men in income.

Economic hardship seems to lessen concern about societal equality and deepen interest in individual gain. When white middle class America is struggling to maintain its standard of living, minorities find themselves most often alone fighting for civil rights. No longer do the widespread coalitions of the 1960s and 1970s exist which fought for solutions for societal ills. College campuses, once the centers for organized protest and change, have turned to directing students into the mainstream and teaching them saleable skills for the job market. In short, apathy and lack of organization weaken the civil rights struggle of the 1980s.

Anti-civil rights sentiment has been manifested recently in the attitude of those on Capitol Hill. Many Reagan administration officials exhibit lukewarm attitudes toward civil rights legislation, while others have tampered with the administrative process so that civil rights legislation has changed in scope and emphasis.

Thomas Sowell, a black economic policy advisor to Reagan, personifies this attitude. Sowell believes that culture, not discrimination, has set the black race back in American society. Furthermore, Sowell advocates abolishing affirmative action, the minimum wage and other government regulatory measures which historically have ensured a measure of equality.

The administration's stance on the Voting Rights Act again illustrates the changing scope of civil rights legislation. While almost all persons supported some form of the Voting Rights Act of 1965, many versions of the bill significantly diluted its power. The Reagan administration supported an amendment to the Section 5 preclearance proviso, which would have allowed jurisdictions with substantial records of compliance to "bail out" from under the act.

Finally, important changes have taken place in government agencies that administer civil rights legislation. The EEOC was left, for a substantial period of time, without commissioners or a chairperson. Those nominated for these positions have either questionable or deplorable civil rights records or lack the administrative ability to run such a large agency.

The Office of Federal Contract Compliance (OFCCP) suffered drastic staff cuts and new administrative guidelines on the number of contractors covered greatly limit the scope of its jurisdiction. Under the new guidelines, unless a contractor does $50,000 worth of business and has at least 100 employees, the employer would escape the inspection of OFCCP. This new provision allows the escape of literally thousands of contractors heretofore covered.

Business has traditionally fought government regulation in the workplace. One business attorney argued, "I think the pendulum has swung too far in favor of the employee. It is too easy for people to believe they have been discriminated against and use the Commission as a way to harass their employer." Business' fight against civil rights legislation is no different. The following are allegations made by business concerns against federal guidelines:

° Current Title VII Federal Law, OFCCP, and state civil rights laws place an expensive burden on businesses to defend themselves from non-meritorious claims of discrimination.

° The amount of paperwork, research and record keeping that must be undertaken to meet government compliance is time-consuming, redundant and expensive.

° Racism is being created, not deleted, by government-imposed "Affirmative Action Quotas" and guidelines on employee selection.

° Frivolous claims could be cut in half by shifting burdens of proof onto those who file charges.

° Employees only file charges to harass their former employers.

Increasingly, a two-tiered system of justice and access to justice is becoming apparent. While many of the notable achievements of the last two decades remain intact at the legislative level, at the administrative level -- the level of access and implementation -- there is disintegration and disrepair.

WHAT STATES CAN DO

Stronger Civil Rights Laws

° States should pass stronger civil rights legislation.
  These new, tougher laws should set tougher penalties for
  discrimination and serve to discourage people from
  discriminating

° States should strengthen state laws prohibiting discrimination in housing, employment and public accommodation.
  In these three areas, states must have the power to initiate
  a complaint without an aggrieved party filing a complaint.

° States should be allowed to seek punitive damages in discrimination cases, so that aggrieved parties can seek
  equitable remedy in both state and federal courts. Particularly in the areas of housing and public accommodation,
  existing state laws, for the most part, don't allow the
  types of remedial damages that would discourage such
  discrimination.

° States should broaden the umbrella of coverage in existing employment discrimination laws, to include small
  companies, large subcontractors and personnel placement
  agencies since they often contribute to employment discrimination.

° States should strengthen and incorporate into state civil
  service laws mechanisms to address civil rights complaints
  through in-house grievance procedures. Inclusive in these
  procedures would be jurisdiction over unjust and discrimi-
  natory practices based upon race, sex, disability, age,
  national origin and sexual harassment.

State Civil Rights Agencies

° States should increase funding and staffing of state and
  local civil rights agencies. Also the staff should be
  better trained to deal effectively with the business
  community in seeking compliance with existent laws.

FOR FURTHER INFORMATION

Publications

Affirmative Action After Bakke, Walter B. Connolly, Jr., Edmond J. Dilworth, Jr., Daniel E. Leach, 1978. Available from Law & Business, Inc., 757 Third Ave., New York, NY 10017.

Affirmative Action For the Handicapped. A Handbook for Employment Opportunity Specialist of the Office of Federal Contract Compliance Programs, U.S. Department of Labor, Washington, D.C., April, 1980.

Dealing With Employment Discrimination, Richard Peres, 1978, Available from McGraw-Hill Book Company, New York, NY.

Labor Law Reports Employment Practices, Commerce Clearing House, Inc., 4025 W. Peterson Avenue, Chicago, IL 60646.

Organizations

CASH (Committee Against Sexual Harassment), 65 S. 4th St., Columbus, OH, 43215 (614) 224-9121.

OHIO GOVERNOR'S COMMITTEE ON EMPLOYMENT OF THE HANDICAPPED, 4656 Heaton Rd., Columbus, OH, 43229 (614) 466-8474.

NATIONAL ASSOCIATION FOR THE ADVANCEMENT OF COLORED PEOPLE, National Office, 1970 Broadway, New York, NY 10019.

NATIONAL ORGANIZATION FOR WOMEN, 425 13th St., N.W., Washington, D.C., 20004 (202) 347-2279.

NINE TO FIVE: A NATIONAL ORGANIZATION OF WORKING WOMEN, 1224 Huron Rd., Cleveland, OH, 44115 (216) 566-9308.

WOMEN'S NETWORK, 39 East Market, 5th Floor, Akron, OH, 44308 Kathy Stierhoff, Executive Director.

Prepared by Michael Samuels.

Women

BACKGROUND FACTS

The majority of women today are in the labor force. More than half of all children have working mothers.

Working women make less than men in every job at every educational level.

The median wage for all permanent, full-time women workers in 1981 was $12,172; for men it was $20,682; for women heading a household without a husband, $10,000.

The number of working women who are poor or "near poor" is large and growing. Most working women (three out of five) earn less than $10,000 a year. One out of three full-time working women earns less than $7,000.

Thirty-five percent of women workers are found in only 25 of 440 job categories. They work in sex-segregated occupational lines at rates of pay which do not equate comparable wages to comparable work.

There are now 8.2 million female-headed families and the number is growing ten times as fast as male-headed families. Female headed households represent 16 percent of all families, but half of all poor families.

Women are on the lowest rungs of the economic ladder. Only one percent earn more than $25,000 per year.

Minority women face the double burden of race and sex discrimination. Women in general earn approximately 59 cents for every dollar earned by white men. Full-time black women workers however, earn only about 54 cents while Hispanic women earn only 49 cents.

Between 12 and 15 million women over the age of 35 are displaced homemakers; they are either divorced, widowed or have been abandoned by their husbands.

Only ten states have Constitutional protection for women. State inheritance taxes, tax law and the property rights of husbands and wives discriminate against women.

THE PROBLEM

Women make up a majority of the population, yet until very recently their problems, needs and aspirations were ignored by federal, state and local government. In the 1960s and 1970s a new sensitivity developed -- encouraged by the rising political power of the women's vote -- and a number of formal and informal barriers were eliminated that prohibited women's full right to participate equally.

However, the conservative and traditional political forces that came to power with the election of Ronald Reagan in 1980 seem committed to reversing many of these gains. Most telling was the administration's role in preventing the ratification of the Equal Rights Amendment. Equally bad for women are the budget and program cutbacks presented by the administration to Congress.

The Reagan administration budgets demands sacrifices from all, but the major burden of sacrifice continues to fall on women.

Examined individually, the cuts are harmful to women. In combination, the budget cuts are devastating. For example, not only are funds for training decreased, but child care support is being withdrawn; grants and loans for independent students are being cut; food programs for women, infants and school children are being eliminated. Each action diminishes opportunities for women and threatens the stability and health of the American family.

Women are vitally important to the American economy. However, while women are working in increasing numbers, the salaries they receive are all too frequently not comparable to the salaries men receive for the same job.

In 1955, women earned 64 percent as much as men; in 1980 women earned 59 percent as much as men. During the 1960s both the Civil Rights Act and the Equal Employment Opportunities Act were passed. Obviously enactment of these two laws has had no effect on the widening wage differential.

Out of this dilemma has come a phrase which most advocates for women feel will be the most pressing women's issue of the 1980s: equal pay for comparable worth. The comparable worth theory holds that whole classes of jobs, such as clerical positions, traditionally have been considered "women's work" and as a result, have been undervalued and underpaid.

Historical reasons for this undervaluation of women's jobs are complex. Those opposed to the idea of comparable worth blame women's "temporary" status in the workforce. She works until she marries or if married, she works to maintain a standard of living or to help out.

Another argument is that pay for a job is determined in the marketplace. Although in most communities there exists a shortage of both secretaries and registered nurses, salaries have not risen appreciably for either profession. In fact, in a comparable worth suit brought against the city and county of Denver by city-county nurses, it was pointed out that intensive care nurses make less than tree trimmers, painters or tire-service men. The nurses lost the court case when the judge ruled that their claim was "pregnant with the possibility of disrupting the entire economic system of the United States."

A major reason such disparity is allowed to continue in this country is that biased or dual classification systems are allowed to be used to measure job worth. Tasks and conditions found primarily in men's jobs are given more compensatory weight than tasks and conditions found predominately in women's jobs.

The majority of women in the labor force are not "comfortable." Most are struggling to keep their heads above water and to provide the basic needs (food, clothing and shelter) for their families.

Many of these women -- known as the "working poor" -- are confronting a difficult decision. If they stay in the workforce and continue to strive toward self-sufficiency, under Reagan regulations they will soon be unable to qualify for benefits which protect their families from illness, malnutrition, etc. The only real option for many is to leave the workforce and become totally dependent on public financial assistance, Medicaid and food stamps.

Also, many women are not in the workforce. Millions of middle-aged and elderly women are separated, divorced or widowed. They dedicated most of their lives to the role of homemaker. They have skills which are valuable but rarely seen as marketable. They have responsibility for themselves and often for dependent children. With a low percentage receiving alimony, pensions, survivor's benefits or inherited wealth, they have few choices. Age discrimination in the marketplace then compounds the problems experienced by these displaced homemakers.

WHAT STATES CAN DO

Pay Equity

° States should mandate its civil service department to evaluate the state workforce with regard to occupational segregation, by race and sex, the skills required for each occupation, and the salary level; and develop a report with recommended changes in categories, skill requirements and salary levels to achieve pay equity.

Removing Economic Bias

° States should pass legislation requiring insurance companies to use only single sex tables in determining premiums and benefits.

° States should require state and local public employee pension funds to give divorced spouses property rights in any pension benefits after 10 years of married life.

Children and Child Care

° States should enact legislation developing comprehensive programs for maternal and child health including health maintenance, immunization and nutrition to make up for cutbacks in those federal programs.

° States should create a special blue ribbon commission to survey the child care needs of the state and propose concrete recommendations to meet the needs of state and private employees.

Education

° States should require the State Department of Education to develop bias-free curriculum and textbooks for introduction throughout school systems in the state.

Constitutional Amendments

° States should pass resolutions requesting that the Congress pass a new federal Equal Rights Amendment.

° States should ratify the federal Equal Rights Amendment when it passes Congress and is submitted to the states for ratification.

° States should amend their own state constitutions to include the Equal Rights Amendment.

° States should oppose ratification of any federal Constitutional amendment that would give the states or Congress the right to limit or prohibit abortions.

FOR FURTHER INFORMATION

Publications

Equal Pay for Work of Comparable Worth: An Annotated
Bibliography of the Business and Professional Women's Foundation.
American Library Association, 50 East Huron Street, Chicago,
IL 60611 (312) 944-6780.

The Female-Male Earnings Gap: A Review of Employment and
Earnings Issues, September, 1982, U.S. Department of Labor,
Bureau of Labor Statistics, Report 673, Washington, D.C. 20212.

Inequality of Sacrifice: The Impact of the Reagan Budget
on Women, National Education Association, 1201 16th Street,
N.W., Washington, DC 20036 (202) 822-7300.

Manual on Pay Equity, Raising Wages for Women's Work,
$8.95 from the Conference on Alternative State and Local
Policies, 2000 Florida Avenue, N.W., Washington, DC 20009
(202) 387-6030.

The Spirit of Houston, The First National Women's Conference, March, 1978, National Commission on the Observance
of International Women's Year, U. S. Government Printing
Office, Washington, DC 20402.

"...To Form a More Perfect Union...," Justice for
American Women, Report of the National Commission on the
Observance of International Women's Year, 1976. U. S. Govern-
ment Printing Office, Washington, DC 20402.

Organizations

NATIONAL COMMITTEE ON PAY EQUITY, 1201 16th Street, N.W.,
Suite 422, Washington, D.C. 20036 (202) 822-7304.
Joy Ann Grune, Director.

NATIONAL ORGANIZATION FOR WOMEN, 425 13th Street, N.W.,
Washington, D.C. 20004 (202) 347-2279. Judy Goldsmith,
President.

NATIONAL WOMEN'S LAW CENTER, 1751 N Street, N.W., Washington,
D.C. 20036 (202) 872-0670. Nancy Duff Campbell.

NINE TO FIVE: A NATIONAL ORGANIZATION OF WORKING WOMEN,
1224 Huron Road, Cleveland, OH 44115 (216) 566-9308. Karen
Nussbaum.

WOMEN'S EQUITY ACTION LEAGUE, 805 15th Street, N.W., Suite
822, Washington, D.C. 20005 (202) 638-1961. Pat Reuss,
Legislative Director.

Prepared by Linda Tarr-Whelan.

National Issues

Constitutional Amendments

BACKGROUND FACTS

The U.S. Constitution is an impressive document.

The Constitution has stood the test of time. It has served the nation well as the framework for a governmental system that has had to confront many varied situations and crises in our history.

Still, the framers of the Constitution understood that even the best-crafted document in the world would need to be modified occasionally to meet changing societal needs. They therefore included amending procedures that offer two routes for proposing amendments and two routes for ratifying them.

Since it was written in 1787, the U.S. Constitution has been amended 26 times. Many of these expanded the rights and obligations for American citizens. The Fourteenth Amendment, for example, gave freed slaves the right to vote, and the Nineteenth, passed in 1920, extended suffrage to all American women. In some instances, constitutional amendments were adopted to bring about greater efficiency and democracy in government (such as those dealing with the succession of office and the direct election of federal legislators).

The Constitution (Article V) provides two routes for proposing amendments and two routes for ratifying them. Amendments can be proposed by a two-thirds affirmative vote of Congress; or, by a constitutional convention, called by Congress, at the request of two-thirds (34) of the state legislatures. Amendments initiated by either process can then be ratified either by the state legislatures or state conventions in three-fourths (38) of the states in order to achieve final adoption. Of the 26 constitutional amendments adopted so far, all have been approved first by Congress and then by the states.

A constitutional convention has not been called since the nation's founders met in Philadelphia in the late 18th century to initially amend the Articles of Confederation and ended up drafting an entirely new Constitution. While several attempts since then have been made to call a convention, all have failed.

THE PROBLEM

In all likelihood, one of the biggest set of issues that America's state legislatures will face in the next several years will be constitutional amendments. State legislators will face politically controversial and even explosive votes regarding if and how the United States Constitution should be amended.

On the one hand, the New Right is proposing constitutional amendments in three key areas: requiring a balanced budget, permitting prayer in the public schools and prohibiting abortion. These issues could reach the state legislatures in 1983 or 1984 if Congress approves them. In addition, the New Right is also trying to pass the balanced budget amendment by calling a Constitutional Convention.

On the other hand, women's, civil rights, labor and other organizations have reintroduced the Equal Rights Amendment into Congress. If Congress passes it again, the state legislatures could possibly receive that in 1983 as well.

The New Right-inspired amendments represent an attempt to make constitutional issues out of partisan social or political policy issues. This is the case with proposed amendments calling for prayer in the schools, an end to school busing and the outlawing of abortions. In addition, the amendment calling for a balanced federal budget represents an attempt to alter the Constitution to provide a temporary political solution to questions of federal fiscal policy.

"Balanced" Budget. Congress considered such a constitutional amendment for submission to the state legislatures during the 97th Congress and will almost certainly do so again during the 98th.

Conservative supporters of a constitutional amendment requiring a balanced budget are also trying another strategy to get their amendment approved. They have gone to the states directly, asking them to call on Congress to call a Constitutional Convention to approve the amendment. Thirty-four states are needed; they now have 31.

Apart from the merits of the issues, the Constitutional Convention raises many legal and constitutional questions. Critics of the Constitutional Convention charge that without established guidelines on how many amendments can be raised, proponents of specific political views could turn the convention into a free-for-all that could leave the entire Constitution up for grabs.

School Prayer. President Reagan submitted a proposed constitutional amendment on prayer in the public schools in May 1982. The Senate held hearings in the summer of 1982, but the measure died on the floor after having failed a number of cloture votes. The President has already resubmitted the same bill to the 98th Congress, where it awaits committee hearings and other action. If supporters could get it out of committee, the amendment could pass the House and the Senate in this session of Congress.

The campaign behind this amendment has been described by some as an attempt to launch a "crusade to recover the Holy Grail from the un-Christian Supreme Court." This highly charged, political measure has been attacked by conservatives and liberals alike.

The amendment clearly is an attempt by right wing and in many cases, fundamentalist Christian groups to sponsor group prayer in the schools; prayer that by many opinions would impose one religious standard over another. This was often the case in the pre-Supreme Court decision days, when Jewish children, among other religious minorities, were often subjected to recitation of the Lord's Prayer in a majority Christian classroom.

Prohibition on Abortion. In every session of Congress since the U.S. Supreme Court decision of 1973 legalizing abortion, legislation or proposed constitutional amendments have been introduced to effectively overturn that decision.

In the Senate a number of proposed constitutional amendments which failed in the 97th Congress have been reintroduced in the 98th. Senator Jesse Helms (R-NC) has introduced two constitutional amendment proposals to outlaw abortion. One, the "Paramount Human Life Amendment," gives "paramount right to life to each human being from the moment of fertilization." The other, the "Unity Human Life Amendment," says: "With respect to the right to life guaranteed to persons by the fifth and fourteenth amendments to the Constitution, the word 'person' applies to all human beings...including their unborn offspring..." Both these proposals have been placed on the Senate calendar and have been sent to the Judiciary Committee for action.

In addition, Senator Orrin Hatch (R-Utah), has reintroduced his "Human Life Federalism Amendment," which he introduced but withdrew from consideration in the 97th Congress. The proposal would amend the Constitution by affirming that both Congress and the states have the power to regulate and/or prohibit abortion. The measure may be taken up by the Judiciary Committee early in the spring of 1983.

Equal Rights Amendment. The ERA was first passed by Congress in 1972 and was defeated June 30, 1982, lacking three states for ratification. The ERA was reintroduced in Congress in July 1982 and Congress will consider it again in 1983. There is the possibility that it could reach the state legislatures in 1983 or 1984.

WHAT STATES CAN DO

Balanced Budget

° State legislatures should reject the proposed constitutional
   amendments requiring a "balanced budget" if Congress
   passes one and submits it to the states.

° State legislatures which have passed resolutions calling
   for a constitutional convention for a balanced budget or other
   issues should rescind their resolution.

° State legislatures which have not passed resolutions
   calling for a constitutional convention should reject any
   or future attempts to do so.

School Prayer

° State legislatures should reject any proposed amendment on
   legalizing organized school prayer if Congress passes
   such an amendment and submits it to the states.

Abortion

° State legislatures should reject any proposed constitutional
   amendment which would allow the Congress or the states to
   prohibit or limit a woman's right to choose if Congress
   passes such an amendment and submits it to the states.

Equal Rights Amendment

° State legislatures should ratify the Equal Rights Amendment
   if Congress passes the amendment and submits it to the
   states.

° State legislatures should pass resolutions in support of
   the ERA and send their resolution to Washington urging Congress to pass the ERA and send it back out to the states
   for ratification.

FOR FURTHER INFORMATION

Balanced Budget

AFL-CIO, 815 16th Street, N.W., Washington, D.C.   20006
(202) 637-5289.

COMMITTEE TO PRESERVE THE CONSTITUTION, 225 West 34th Street,
Suite 1500, New York, NY 10001.

LEAGUE OF WOMEN VOTERS, 1730 M Street, N.W., Washington,
D.C. 20036 (202) 429-1965.

NATIONAL EDUCATION ASSOCIATION, 1201 16th Street, N.W.,
Washington, D.C. 20036 (202) 833-4000.

Constitutional Convention

COMMITTEE TO PRESERVE THE CONSTITUTION, 225 West 34th Street,
Suite 1500, New York, NY 10001.

Abortion

NATIONAL ABORTION RIGHTS ACTION LEAGUE, 1424 K Street, N.W.,
Washington, D.C. 20005 (202) 347-7774.

PLANNED PARENTHOOD FEDERATION OF AMERICA, 1220 19th Street,
N.W., #303, Washington, D.C. 20036 (202) 347-8500.

RELIGIOUS COALITION FOR ABORTION RIGHTS, 100 Maryland Avenue,
N.E., Washington, D.C. 20002 (202) 543-7032.

School Prayer

AMERICAN CIVIL LIBERTIES UNION, 132 West 43rd Street, New
York, NY 10036 (212) 944-9800.

AMERICANS UNITED FOR SEPARATION OF CHURCH AND STATE, 8120
Fenton Street, Silver Spring, MD 20910 (301) 589-3707

NATIONAL EDUCATION ASSOCIATION, 1201 16th Street, N.W.,
Washington, D.C. 20036 (202) 833-4000.

Equal Rights Amendment

LEAGUE OF WOMEN VOTERS, 1730 M Street, N.W., Washington,
D.C. 20036 (202) 429-1965.

NATIONAL ORGANIZATION FOR WOMEN, 425 13th Street, N.W.,
Washington, D.C. 20004 (202) 347-2279.

NATIONAL WOMEN'S POLITICAL CAUCUS, 1411 K Street, N.W.,
Washington, D.C. 20005 (202) 347-3078.

Prepared by Linda Tarr-Whelan and Andrea DiLorenzo.

Nuclear Weapons Freeze

BACKGROUND FACTS

In just 30 minutes, every major city in the Northern Hemisphere could be destroyed by the arsenal of 50,000 nuclear weapons possessed by the United States and the Soviet Union.

Yet over the next decade, both countries plan to build approximately 20,000 more nuclear warheads, missiles and aircraft.

These rapidly escalating numbers have alarmed hundreds of thousands of Americans. Growing concern about the threat of a nuclear holocaust has led to a groundswell of support for a "freeze" of existing U.S./Soviet nuclear weapons. This proposal has aroused more American support than any arms control issue since the end of World War II.

Areas of "high risk" -- likely targets of a Soviet nuclear attack -- are located in every state in the nation. Industrialized urban centers and areas with major military installations are primary targets.

The freeze movement began to gather momentum in November 1980. Efforts have been directed on a state-by-state basis with activity occurring at each level of government.

Legislatures in Connecticut, Delaware, Hawaii, Iowa, Maine, Massachusetts, Minnesota, New York, Oregon, Vermont and Wisconsin have passed freeze resolutions, as well as the Kansas, Missouri, North Carolina, and Pennsylvania Houses of Representatives, the California State Assembly and the Alaska, Illinois and Maryland State Senates. In the November 1982 election, referendums passed in California, Massachusetts, Michigan, Montana, New Jersey, North Dakota, Oregon, Rhode Island and Wisconsin.

At the local level, 348 city councils, 444 New England town meetings and 64 county councils have passed freeze resolutions. The U.S. Conference of Mayors, the National Conference of Black Mayors and the National Conference of State Legislatures have all passed endorsement resolutions.

On January 26, 1983, Senators Edward Kennedy (D-MA) and Mark O. Hatfield (R-OR) introduced Senate Joint Resolution 2, calling for a "mutual and verifiable freeze" on the testing, deployment and production of warheads and delivery systems with "major, mutual reductions" to follow the freeze. Thirty-four co-sponsors have signed the resolution.

THE PROBLEM

Arms control and nuclear war are two of the most critical issues facing our nation. Public officials at all levels of government are becoming actively involved.

Although public support for a freeze resolution is now substantial and growing, the idea of a weapons freeze is not new. Both the Johnson and Nixon administrations considered freeze proposals and the idea resurfaced in 1979 during the Carter administration, when the President proposed a freeze on production and deployment of nuclear weapons to the Soviet Premier, Leonid Brezhnev.

The freeze movement has grown rapidly since 1980 despite critics' attempts to stop it. There are two major arguments used by opponents of the freeze. One is that the United States trails the Soviet Union in nuclear weapons strength, and that a freeze would leave the U.S. at a strategic dis-advantage. This argument, however, ignores an important point: while the Soviet Union has a greater number of inter-continental ballistic missiles and more throw-weight (total size of payload) than the United States, the U.S. has a greater number of warheads than the Soviet Union.

In addition to the United States' lead in the number of warheads, the U.S. maintains an unchallenged advantage in both sea-launched ballistic missiles, which are less vulnerable than land-based missiles and in heavy bombers, which are now being equipped with highly effective cruise missiles. The superiority of the U.S. in these two legs of the strategic triad compensates for both the vulnerability of our land-based missiles and for the Soviet lead in total missiles and throw-weight.

Freeze opponents also argue that the Soviet Union has more intermediate range forces in Europe than NATO. This is true, however, if only ground-based missiles are counted; if U.S. and British sea- and air-launched missiles are included, NATO forces are brought to parity with Soviet forces in Europe.

The second major argument used by freeze opponents is that the Soviet Union cannot be trusted to comply with the freeze and that the U.S. does not have adequate means to verify compliance. (The resolution calls for an agreement based on mutual verification in all stages of testing, production and deployment of nuclear weapons.)

Verification technology does exist and is reliable. A freeze on the testing of delivery systems can be monitored by U.S. satellites and a freeze on the testing of warheads can be monitored by seismographic instruments. In the case of cruise missiles -- designed to fly beneath ground radar -- it must be noted that only the United States has developed them and that if the Soviet Union should develop and test them, they can be monitored by satellite surveillance and reconnaissance planes.

A freeze on deployment of new weapons is the easiest aspect of arms control to monitor: delivery systems are difficult to conceal from overhead surveillance; bombers, land-based missiles and submarine-launched missiles are readily visible to satellites; and cruise missile deployment can be checked through controls on the number and loading capacity of their launch planes. (This procedure was success-fully incorporated into the SALT II agreement.) Sea-launched cruise missiles are not presently being deployed and because their deployment would be extremely difficult if not impossible to verify, an immediate freeze on all nuclear weapons deployment would forestall this serious arms control problem.

A freeze on production is perhaps the most difficult aspect of arms control to verify, although it is still possible. Freeze advocates contend that the U.S. has sufficient knowledge of Soviet production plant locations to enable it to monitor activity by infra-red sensors on satellites that detect the heat emitted from active plants. On-site inspection would verify a plant's deactivation and thereafter, satellite observation would detect re-established production at a deactivated plant. Attempts to build new plants can also be discovered through such means.

WHAT STATES CAN DO

° States should pass resolutions calling for an immediate freeze and mutually verifiable reductions in the testing, production and further deployment of nuclear weapons, missiles and other delivery systems in the U.S. and Soviet Union.

° States should pass legislation that would refuse to allocate state funds, staff time or facilities to civil defense planning. Such state resources should only be earmarked for other types of emergency disaster situations.

° States should pass resolutions calling upon Congress to divert tax dollars spent on nuclear weapons and other unnecessary military spending to jobs and other human services.

° States should modify their economic development plans towards diversifying economies that significantly depend on military contracts. States should consider matching funds with state military contractors to finance feasibility studies for such diversification.

° States should change their regulations and agreements with the Federal Emergency Management Agency (FEMA) to redefine an emergency to include those created by toxic and hazardous waste dumps. Funds originally allocated to crisis relocation should be rededicated to meeting such civil emergencies.

° States should require the state's economic development department to prepare an annual study of the impact of military spending on the state's economy, including the percentage of each citizen's taxes that go to the military. This study should be published in the state's major newspapers and a summary of it included in state income tax forms mailed to all citizens.

° States should pass an annual resolution recommending a proper share of the federal budget between competing priorities. Such a resolution would recommend a suggested percentage that defense expenditures should make up of the total federal budget.

° States should create an office of economic conversion in the state planning or economic development department. This office should provide assistance to firms in that state who want to move from military contracts to the civilian market.

FOR FURTHER INFORMATION

Publications

Beyond the Nuclear Freeze: An Agenda for the States, Lee Webb, 1983. Model Agenda, $2.50 from the Conference on Alternative State and Local Policies.

Civilian Defense from Nuclear War Information Packet, 1982, Civil Defense Awareness, 22 Lowell Street, Cambridge, MA 02133.

Freeze Fact Sheets, Nuclear Weapons Freeze Campaign, National Clearinghouse, 4144 Lindel, Suite 404, St. Louis, MO 63108, $.07 each. Five fact sheets on a variety of freeze and nuclear issues.

Freeze! How Can You Prevent Nuclear War? Senator Edward Kennedy and Senator Mark Hatfield, 1982. Bantam Publishing Co. $3.50.

A "Jobs with Peace" Budget: A Model Resolution for States and Cities, Dan Ruben, 1983. Legislative Brief, $2.50 from the Conference on Alternative State and Local Policies.

Questions and Answers on the Soviet Threat and National Security. $ .75. American Friends Service Committee, 1501 Cherry St., Philadelphia, PA 19102.

Rejecting Crisis Relocation Plans: The Cambridge, Massachusetts Ordinance, $2.50 from the Conference on Alternative State and Local Policies.

Organizations

CENTER FOR DEFENSE INFORMATION, 122 Maryland Avenue N.E., Washington, D.C. 20002 (202) 484-9490.

COMMITTEE FOR NATIONAL SECURITY, 2000 P Street, N.W., Washington, D.C. 20036 (202) 833-3140. A nonprofit, nonpartisan leadership group which promotes debate on the nature of national security and how best to achieve it.

CONFERENCE ON ALTERNATIVE STATE AND LOCAL POLICIES, 2000 Florida Avenue N.W., Washington, D.C. 20009 (202) 387-6030.

NUCLEAR WEAPONS FREEZE CAMPAIGN NATIONAL CLEARINGHOUSE, 4144 Lindell Blvd., Suite 404, St. Louis, MO 63108 (314) 533-1169. Encourages and assists "freeze" activists throughout the nation.

PHYSICIANS FOR SOCIAL RESPONSIBILITY, P.O.Box 144, 23 Main Street, Watertown, MA 02172 (617) 491-2754. An organization of health professionals and concerned citizens.

Prepared by Victoria Baldwin, Ann Cahn and Lou Kerestesy.

List of Contributors

Victoria Baldwin (NUCLEAR WEAPONS FREEZE) was a research
 assistant at the Joint Economic Committee of the U.S.
 Congress and is currently studying at the University of
 California, Los Angeles.

Joe Belden (FARM AND FOOD POLICY) is an agricultural policy
 consultant.

Barbara Bode (CHILD CARE) is President of the Children's
 Foundation.

Fred Branfman (HIGH TECHNOLOGY) is Director of Research for
 the Institute for National Strategy.

Jeff Brummer (UTILITIES) is Utilities Clearinghouse
 Coordinator with the Electric Utilities Project of the
 Environmental Action Foundation.

Ann Cahn (NUCLEAR WEAPONS FREEZE) is executive director of
 the Committee for National Security.

Joanna Chusid (THE ELDERLY) is senior Legislative Assistant
 at the National Council of Senior Citizens.

Worth Kitson Cooley (CHILD SUPPORT ENFORCEMENT) is Director
 of the Child Support Enforcement Project at the Children's
 Foundation.

Elliott Currie (CRIMINAL JUSTICE) is Research Associate at
 the Center for Study of Law and Society at the University of
 California at Berkeley.

Andrea DiLorenzo (CONSTITUTIONAL AMENDMENTS, PUBLIC EDUCATION)
 is a legislative information specialist with the National
 Education Association.

Ann Evans (COOPERATIVES) is the President of the California
 Co-op Federation and the Mayor Pro Tempore of Davis, California.

Donald Fraher (HANDGUN CONTROL) is Legislative Director for
 Handgun Control, Inc.

John Froines (WORKPLACE SAFETY AND HEALTH) is former Vermont
 Director of Occupational Health and former Deputy Director
 of the National Institute for Occupational Safety and
 Health. He is currently a faculty member of the School of
 Public Health at the University of California, Los Angeles.

Leonard Goldberg (HOUSING) is a legislative staff specialist for California Assemblyman Tom Bates.

Derek Hansen (SMALL BUSINESS) is President of Derek Hansen and Associates, Inc.

Marilee Hanson (HOUSING) is a housing consultant in Oakland, California.

Edward Hopkins (WATER AND SEWERS) is Research Director of the Clean Water Action Project.

Robert Hunter (INSURANCE) is Executive Director of the National Insurance Consumers Organization.

David Jones (PLANT CLOSINGS, STUDENTS) is Editor of Ways and Means at the Conference on Alternative State and Local Policies.

William Jordan (NUCLEAR ENERGY) is a partner with the Washington, D.C. public interest law firm of Harmon & Weiss.

Deborah Kaplan (CITIZENS WITH DISABILITIES) is a staff attorney at the Disability Rights Education and Defense Fund.

Lou Kerestesy (NUCLEAR WEAPONS FREEZE) is an intern at the Committee for National Security.

Peter Lafen (ENVIRONMENTAL PROTECTION) is Transportation Counsel at Friends of the Earth.

Linda Lampkin (PUBLIC EMPLOYEES) is Director of Research at the American Federation of State, County and Municipal Employees.

Thomas Leatherwood (PENSION FUND INVESTMENT) is Executive Director of the Public Pension Investment Project.

James Lewis (TOXICS) is former editor of Exposure, the publication of the Waste and Toxic Substances project of the Environmental Action Foundation.

Peter Manikas (CORRUPTION AND WASTE) is Legislative Counsel and chief of the Washington, D.C. office of the Better Government Association.

Richard Munson (ENERGY CONSERVATION) is former Executive Director of Solar Lobby.

Barbara Pape (BLOCK GRANTS) is a research associate at the public policy consulting firm of Chambers Associates.

Anthony Robbins (HEALTH CARE) is former Director of the National Institute for Occupational Safety and Health and is President of the American Public Health Association.

Michael Samuels (CIVIL RIGHTS) is Executive Director of the Ohio Civil Rights Commission.

William Schweke (LABOR LEGISLATION, PLANT CLOSINGS) is Managing Editor of The Entrepreneurial Economy at the Corporation for Enterprise Development.

Ken Silver (TOXICS) is a toxics specialist for the Waste and Toxic Substances Project of the Environmental Action Foundation.

Richard Spohn (CONSUMER PROTECTION) is the former Director of the California Department of Consumer Affairs, now a partner in the San Francisco office of the law firm of Nossaman, Guthner, Knox and Elliott.

Larry Swift (BANKING) is President of the Woodstock Institute.

Linda Tarr-Whelan (CONSTITUTIONAL AMENDMENTS, PUBLIC EDUCATION, WOMEN) is Director of Government Relations at the National Education Association.

Lori Weinstein (CHILD CARE) is the Family Day Care Advocacy Director of the Children's Foundation.

David Wilhelm (TAX REFORM) is a research specialist with the Public Employee Department of the AFL-CIO.

Robert Zdenek (COMMUNITY ECONOMIC DEVELOPMENT) is President of the National Congress for Community Economic Development.

David Zwick (WATER AND SEWERS) is Executive Director of the Clean Water Action Project.